EXPERIENCING GOD'S FORGIVENESS

EXPERIENCING GOD'S FORGIVENESS

THE JOURNEY FROM GUILT TO GLADNESS

JOHN ENSOR

NAVPRESS

BRINGING TRUTH TO LIFE
NavPress Publishing Group
P.O. Box 35001, Colorado Springs, Colorado 80935

The Navigators is an international Christian organization. Our mission is to reach, disciple, and equip people to know Christ and to make Him known through successive generations. We envision multitudes of diverse people in the United States and every other nation who have a passionate love for Christ, live a lifestyle of sharing Christ's love, and multiply spiritual laborers among those without Christ.

NavPress is the publishing ministry of The Navigators. NavPress publications help believers learn biblical truth and apply what they learn to their lives and ministries. Our mission is to stimulate spiritual formation among our readers.

© 1997 by John M. Ensor

Library of Congress Catalog Card Number: 97-3369
ISBN 1-57683-013-6

Cover illustration: Chris Sheban/E. W. Inman

Most of the anecdotal illustrations in this book are true to life and are included with the permission of the persons involved. All other illustrations are composites of real situations, and any resemblance to people living or dead is coincidental.

Some words are italic to highlight the author's emphasis.

Unless otherwise identified, all Scripture quotations in this publication are taken from the HOLY BIBLE: NEW INTERNATIONAL VERSION ® (NIV®). Copyright © 1973, 1978, 1984 by International Bible Society. Used by permission of Zondervan Publishing House. All rights reserved. Other versions used include: the New American Standard Bible (NASB), © The Lockman Foundation 1960, 1962, 1963, 1968, 1971, 1972, 1973, 1975, 1977; the New Revised Standard Version (NRSV), copyright 1989, by the Division of Christian Education of the National Council of the Churches of Christ in the USA, used by permission, all rights reserved; and the New King James Version (NKJV), copyright © 1979, 1980, 1982, 1990, Thomas Nelson Inc., Publishers.

Ensor, John M.
   Experiencing God's forgiveness : the journey from guilt to gladness / John M. Ensor.
      p.   cm.
   Includes bibliographical references.
   ISBN 1-57683-013-6 (pbk.)
   1. Forgiveness—Religious aspects—Christianity. 2. Guilt —Religious aspects—Christianity. I. Title.
   BV4647.F55E47   1997
   234'.5—dc21   97-3369
                                                      CIP

Printed in the United States of America
1 2 3 4 5 6 7 8 9 10 11 12 13 14 15 / 00 99 98 97

Contents

To my wife,

Leigh Kristen

*A true partner in the journey from guilt to gladness—
and the greatest evidence of God's blessing on my life.*

Acknowledgments

All the people mentioned in this book are real. They are not composites drawn from numerous sources. With one exception, even their names are real. The exception is in the opening story of Alice. She has left the area, perhaps even the country, and I haven't been able to contact her. The rest have graciously granted me permission to use their names and their stories in order to flesh out the truths of the gospel as we experience it. For this I owe them a great debt of thanks.

I'm also greatly indebted to the people of the former Dorchester Christian Fellowship. Their humble and hungry faith inspired me to search out life-changing truths from Scripture in order that their passion for God might run well along the tracks of God's Word. I owe them much for the challenge they gave me to present deep truths with simplicity and straightforwardness.

I'm also thankful to peers in the ministry, Pastors David Bissett, Dana Olson, and John Piper, for critiquing this book. Their standards of accuracy and clarity certainly helped make this book better than originally written. Liz Heaney, my editor at NavPress, has been invaluable to me in cutting down on my excess verbiage and forcing me to think through each sentence and paragraph from the readers' vantage point. Any shortcomings that remain are my own. I'm also grateful for the steady encouragement of Christian friends at Camp Spofford, New Hampshire, especially Gary Johnson and Bonnie Rise, Tom and Judy Larson, and Barbara Moretti. Their generosity and love nurtured this book toward completion.

Finally, the contribution my family made to this book was substantive and sacrificial. My three children, Nathanael, Megan, and Elliot, sacrificed a lot of "Papa time" to this book and never showed any resentment for it. My wife, Kristen, believed when I did not. She pushed when I was stuck. She corrected when I misread. She's prayed that this book produces much gladness toward God. She's eighteen years my helpmate and in writing this book has affirmed for me once again the sweetness of Proverbs 12:4: "An excellent wife is the crown of her husband" (NASB).

Foreword

I am a painfully slow reader. So I must be ruthless in the good things that I choose not to read. I did not begrudge the time it took to read this book. I started it because John Ensor is an admired friend. I finished it because it is a very good book.

I love the God-centeredness of this book. At one point I wrote in the margin, "John's great strength is reasserting the greatness of God in a way so compelling that God-neglecting moderns might feel it." In another place I wrote, "This book is a celebration of the greatness of Christ's work on the cross." And the Cross is not the measure of our worth, but of God's: "Christ's death for us is grounded firmly on the value [God] places on Himself and His own glory as a loving God." The book is a God-entranced vision of glorious forgiveness. "For your name's sake, O Lord, forgive my sins!"

The book succeeds because it is biblical. It is saturated with the Bible. John has a sweeping knowledge of Scripture and interprets it carefully. He would agree that the sieve of human thought is God's thought. So he says, "Test everything by whether it advances or diminishes the glory of God as He reveals Himself in the Bible." And in another place: "Only a truth-soaked mind can reshape our opinions, attitudes, responses, and decisions." It is a vibrantly truth-driven book.

It also succeeds because it is real. It connects with life. John writes with the savvy of one who has seen the legal and justice system from the inside. He has struggled with the most impossible crises. He has lost friends in murder. He has gained friends from converted criminals. He knows the street. He has learned some deep things; "If I come across a man raping a woman, I cannot love both of them in the same way." His God-centeredness grew in abortion wars and drug deals and manifold cases of abuse. What you read here has been tested in fire.

The book succeeds because it is full of compassion and hope. The glory of God is mainly the glory of His mercy. And the way to make it known is to move from guilt to gladness by faith. Under God the persons that count most are the broken, trapped, hopeless sinners. "I want them to become living testimonies to the glory of God's mercy as they experience a transformation from guilt to gladness."

But for all its emphasis on compassion, the book is not sappy. John is Jesus-like in his utter freedom from sentimentality. He is, in fact, strikingly blunt. "Murmuring is God-hatred in the acorn stage." "Our deepest problem is not our woundedness but our waywardness." There is such a thing as "good shame." The wrath of God is "terrible . . . fierce . . . awful." One thing God will not forgive is the "discounting of the work of grace wrought by the Spirit."

Yet for all its bluntness it is a happy book. "To believe means to trust in the work God does for our joy and His glory." "The faith we are to place in God is a glad willingness to trust that He will provide for us everything that will truly make us happy in the long run." John is gripped by the great truth that God is glorified in us when we are satisfied in Him.

For seasoning, the book is strewn with the wisdom of an amazing range of writers: Frederick Buechner, G. K. Chesterton,

Victor Hugo, C. S. Lewis, Robert McCheyne, John Milton, Henri Nouwen, Elie Wiesel, etc. Some are not only penetrating but also entertaining: "Everybody is a tick in search of a dog" (Larry Crabb).

Experiencing God's Forgiveness is God-centered good news. It is the kind of message that will make deep, strong people and deep, strong churches. It will release people from the self-absorbed rationalizations that keep us from the fullest engagement in the global cause of God. So I am hopeful that for God's sake the gladness on the other side of guilt will also be the gladness of the nations—in God.

John Piper, pastor
Bethlehem Baptist Church
Minneapolis, Minnesota
October 30, 1996

Packing for the Journey from Guilt to Gladness

As a pastor and crisis counselor, I meet people every day who are plagued with guilt. They suffer hot flashes of shame, self-loathing, and regret. Usually these feelings arise from some particularly heinous action on their part—something they know was selfish and wrong. They did it and they can't undo it. They feel God can't forgive them—indeed, that they ought not to be forgiven. Some of these people are Christians; some are not. Regardless, they are a bit confused.

Some will attend church on Sunday and offer a friendly greeting. They have their "game face" on, but inside they hope for a word that will *finally* release them. It hasn't come yet, at least in a way they can comprehend. Others feel disqualified from the Christian faith. They no longer believe God could have anything good to say to them.

In the opening chapter of this book, I write about a few of these people. Specifically, I chose to begin with people I know and love who have wrestled with the guilt of premarital sex and the complications that follow. I take a risk in starting here, because people who are not guilty of these things may think this book is not for them. But there are three very good reasons for starting with these *sins of the flesh* rather than the more subtle sins of the heart, such as pride, self-determination, or bitterness.

First, I want guilt-ridden people to know that they are the most forgivable people on the earth, not the most unforgivable. Of all the people on earth, these are the hungriest to taste the forgiveness of God. If I start with anyone else, I fear these guilt-ridden people will think this book is for others and not for them. It's my prayer that this book fall into the hands of people who really think, for *whatever* reason, that "God can never forgive me." I want them to become living testimonies to the glory of God's mercy as they experience a transformation from guilt to gladness. I believe they are in God's cross hairs as the primary target of His great gift. It will produce in them the greatest joy and the most fervent praise to God, just as surely as stars shine brightest against the darkest of nights.

Second, I recognize that the best Christians among us are coming out of an indulgent and perverse culture of sex and violence. These sincere Christians may want to serve God, but they're hamstrung by deeply embedded, secret guilt over some rather unpleasant things that never get discussed in polite Christian circles. Their secrecy and our silence combine to paralyze their walk in Christ. It so stains their consciences that they wonder if the grace of God really extends *that far*. The result is thousands of Christians who think, *If you really knew who I was and what I've done, you wouldn't like me, and you certainly wouldn't ask me to actually do anything radical and challenging as a Christian.*

I want this book to fall into the hands of sincere and serious Christians who want to know the cleansing power and transforming grace of the gospel. It is my hope that, armed with this fuller and richer explanation of the transforming process of God's forgiveness, they will be clothed with the confidence and moral courage needed to wage the war of love against all things that destroy body and soul.

The third reason I start with sins of the flesh is that when it comes to gaining an honest sense of our guilt, outward sins awaken our conscience to sins of the heart. I meet very few people desperate to know the forgiveness of God because of the bitterness they hold against their spouse or the shame they feel for bad-mouthing their boss. No one comes to me in tears over his gluttony or for envying the success of another. True, the love of money, fame, and power has destroyed more people than gazing at *Playboy* magazine, but we tend to hide pornography and flaunt power. That suggests that we sense right and wrong more quickly with our fleshly lusts than we do with the lust of our natural pride.

No one has ever come to me convicted by their lack of concern for the poor, or for failing to visit the sick, even though these sins of omission reflect a lack of love so abominable, Jesus said, as to justify eternal damnation (see Matthew 25:31-46).

Most people first experience guilt over what is self-evidently wicked or socially reinforced as wrong. Then they work back to what is less visible, subtle, and more diabolical. In this book are people guilty of murder and rape, as well as self-righteousness and self-rule, unbelief and unforgiveness. As we trace the true nature of guilt, we will eventually all find ourselves caught in the net. Therefore, I plead for your patience and discernment. Look at the reality and machinations of guilt and liberation at work in the stories I tell and apply them to your own journey. Don't look at the examples and compare yourself with them, for better or worse. You will miss the point completely.

PACKING FOR THE JOURNEY
FROM GUILT TO GLADNESS

In this book I hope to move you along the path from guilt to gladness. In this journey it will be helpful to remember three things.

The Fixed Point of Reference
Every journey is aided by a fixed point of reference. Mine is Colossians 1:21-23. Everything I am trying to say in this book

can be simplified down to these eighty-seven divinely inspired words written by the apostle Paul:

> Once you were alienated from God and were enemies in your minds because of your evil behavior. But now He has reconciled you by Christ's physical body through death to present you holy in His sight, without blemish and free from accusation—if you continue in your faith, established and firm, not moved from the hope held out in the gospel. This is the gospel that you heard and that has been proclaimed to every creature under heaven, and of which I, Paul, have become a servant.

Start here. If you lose your way, return here. When you're finished, come back here. It's our anchor text. I wrote this book in the hope that it will help others know the joy of these words as a heartfelt experience.

The Direction of the Compass

This book is true to the extent that it unremittingly points to the glory of God, as surely as the needle of a compass points to the pole. Test everything here by whether it advances or diminishes the glory of God as He reveals Himself in the Bible. As such, the test is *not* whether this book will help you *feel* better or happier right away. That reduces God to a means to our self-centered fulfillment. Though you may not realize it yet, God is our end as well as our means. We were made to enjoy God. This book is about how to get reconciled with Him so that we can live to the praise of His glory. The magnetic force is God's glory. Follow the needle to that, and you will be unspeakably happy.

Two Sure Guides

When G. K. Chesterton, the wry British Catholic author, was once asked which book he would most like to take along if he knew he was going to be shipwrecked on an island, his immediate response was, "I think I should like to take Thomas' *Guide to Practical Shipbuilding.*" So in our journey we need a practical guidebook. This book aims to point you to that Book. The Bible is an infallible and trustworthy guide, and we will consult it every step of the way. The role of the Holy Spirit in understanding the truth of the Bible is to work on the natural pride and resistance we feel to the truth and to help us cherish and hold fast to the hope offered in the gospel. So, as you read, pray for His truth to be ignited in your heart by the power of the Holy Spirit. God will do a gracious and mighty work.

In putting this book before the public, I am, as Thomas Watson said, "the well-wisher of your soul's happiness."

The Christian Experience of God's Forgiveness

*I will not glory because I am righteous but because I am redeemed,
not because I am clear of sin, but because my sins are forgiven.*
—SAINT AMBROSE

∾

*For what I received I passed on to you as of first importance:
that Christ died for our sins.*
—1 CORINTHIANS 15:3

Alice was twenty-two years old, a self-professing Christian with strong moral values. Raised in a strict Christian home, she was a senior in college and so scared that even after we talked for an hour she was still too afraid to tell me her first name.

"Call me X," she said.

Her crisis? She had fallen into a sexual relationship for the first time. It lasted about four days. Physically and emotionally sickened with guilt, Alice left school. Since she had no place to go, she stayed with her boyfriend. She was also terrified that she might be pregnant. The shame an out-of-wedlock pregnancy would bring to her family was gripping, but the thought of an abortion, which she believed was murder, terrorized her further. She knew she would be aborting herself and her faith too. In this desperate act of self-preservation, God would despise her as she despised herself.

The next day Alice came to see me. A few minutes into our counseling session she startled me by asking, "Are you a Christian?" As the founder and director of three crisis pregnancy centers in the Boston area, my counseling staff and I talk to numerous young women and their "partners" every day.[1] Though we are a Christian service ministry, we do not start our counseling with our values but with the needs of our clients. I had not mentioned God. Still, Alice detected something.

"Yes, I'm a Christian," I answered.

She replied, with eyes fixed on the carpet, "I *used* to be a Christian. But I lost my salvation."

This, too, startled me, and I responded, "How interesting. Just how did you do that?"

Alice explained what I already knew. She believed her premarital sexual activity was wrong—a violation of both her own conscience and the Word of God. What she had done and what she was contemplating doing if she was pregnant were heinous evils in her own mind and worthy of the just condemnation of a righteous God. Doing so, with full knowledge of the truth, would put her beyond the reach of God's forgiveness forever, she thought.

She had already stopped going to church in the previous weeks. "How can I go there and worship God when I know what I've done?" she said. Her closest friend was not a Christian, and Alice had tried to show her what a difference Christ can make in one's life. "But now—I've got no place to say anything to anybody, after what I've done!" She stopped praying too. In truth, she was afraid to pray. "How could God ever forgive me for what I've done?" Alice wept before me. "I've ruined my life!" She felt beyond hope and fearfully guilty.

There are many Alices in the world. Author and speaker Josh McDowell has spoken on campuses around the world for over twenty-five years.[2] He reports,

> Probably the most asked question that I get as I speak to young people around the country is "Can God really love and forgive me?" The question almost always relates to sex and usually to premarital sex. Young people just don't believe that God can forgive them. They think that their sin is too great or that somehow because it's a sexual sin, they'll never be able to feel forgiven.[3]

But there is hope for Alice and all of us, no matter what particular sin now stains our conscience and alienates us from God. There is a reason that the Christian's hope burst on the scene with angelic brilliance announcing, "Do not be afraid. I bring you good news of great joy" (Luke 2:10). The joyful news is this: God can transform our guilt to gladness—even more, He is *glad* to do so.

ANTOINETTE AND RICH

Antoinette and Rich sought the forgiveness of God under very different circumstances. They had lived together for nine years, since they were sixteen years old, and had two children. Rich had spent time in jail for selling drugs. Upon his release he decided to "go straight" and went to work at McDonald's. When Antoinette came to our center, she tested positive for pregnancy and was glad about it. Things were tough, but she wanted another child. During her time of counseling, many things came out: her painful childhood, her reckless youth, her multiple abortions, her recent attendance at a nearby church, her sense of need for God's peace. Her counselor was a kind and discerning Christian. They talked honestly about God's desire that she should know His peace. Antoinette listened intently.

Two months later Antoinette called back. "Pray for me," she begged, "and ask God to forgive me for what I am about to do tomorrow." She was scheduled to terminate her nineteen-week, preborn child in the morning. She had lost her job, Rich couldn't find a second one, and she had grown afraid and depressed. Surely God would understand that having a baby in these circumstances would be too much for her right now, she thought. But if not, He'll listen to my counselor's prayers because she's a serious Christian.

What could we say? We can't call upon a good God to do evil. If we can't trust God to provide a simple job for us, how can we trust Him to solve the problem of our terrible sins? To pray for permission to destroy an innocent life is to make a mockery of the entire Christian faith; it shows contempt for the forgiveness of God and turns it into a license to sin. Antoinette was dangerously confused about God's forgiveness. But many of us are. Under these terms forgiveness is not extended—in fact, I think it angers God that we should even ask. It's like someone asking me for permission to rape my daughter. The very question ignites a holy rage in defense of my daughter and against her assailant.

EVA

Eva is a very young Christian. On a recent visit the subject of our families came up. Family to me is primarily my wife, Kristen, and our three kids, Nathanael, Megan, and Elliot. We were planning a birthday party for Megan later that week. Eva was twenty-three and single, and family for her was the new church she was in. Regarding her immediate family, she sighed and explained, "John, I was ten years old when I started to drink and smoke pot. When I was eleven I did this with my father. He bought me a line of cocaine when I was seventeen. That pretty much explains where I'm coming from."

I almost burst out in tears. What kind of father buys cocaine for his teenage daughter? I long to see my daughter loved and nurtured and confident and healthy, simply because I love her. What kind of evil is this that robs a young girl of fatherly love and treats her to the perverse pleasures of snorting cocaine? Eva spent years on the streets: drugs; alcohol; sexual promiscuity; and lots of pain, confusion, anger, and lostness. I went home and hugged my daughter that night. I felt angry at Eva's father as I told Eva's story to my wife. That man must pay some sort of penalty for what he did to Eva, I fumed. Here forgiveness seems immoral, and a just God would not give it. But is it sinful of me to think so? If so, is it a sin God can forgive? Are my sins less sinful?

SEARCHING OUT THE FORGIVENESS OF GOD

In one of his great novels Fyodor Dostoyevsky asked, "Is there in the whole world a person who would have the right to forgive and could forgive?"[4] Alice felt beyond the forgiveness of

God. Antoinette had a false hope regarding the forgiveness of God. Eva had her first taste of the forgiveness of God—now she would need to extend it to her father. Hearing about Eva's father, and having lived long enough to see many examples of genuine evil committed against innocent people, I wondered again what the limits of forgiveness should rightly be for a holy and just God.

There are *many* probing questions we can ask in our desire to get hold of a biblically based, God-glorifying, heartfelt experience of God's forgiveness. Does God forgive? Does He forgive everyone or only some? Are there degrees of sin? Is speeding to church as bad as adultery? Is slander the same as a slit throat? Does the forgiveness of God go only so far?

Aren't some things unforgivable? If a judge let everybody go, justice would not be served. How can God wink at the wickedness of people and leave them unpunished? Do rapists and murderers sit down in heaven with raped and murdered men, women, and children and say, "Let's all live in harmony?" Is that heaven? Isn't there hell to pay for our sins? And if there is, how can *I* ever escape it?

Will God be more willing to forgive me if I make a sincere effort to reform myself? Will it help if I punish myself in certain ways? How *can* God forgive me for what I've done? I condemn myself, how can God do less?

Can I have any assurance that God has forgiven me? What are the grounds for this assurance? Can I ever live without the painful shame of the past? We'll search the Scriptures to find the answers to all these questions in the pages ahead.

Charles Spurgeon (1834-1892), the famous London preacher of the last century, openly wrestled with these questions in his early years. He had difficulty finding a church that addressed the crucial question of how to experience God's forgiveness. According to his biographer, Arnold Dallimore,

> [Charles] inwardly was in anguish. In latter years, as he looked back upon this terrible time, he said, "I thought I would rather have been a frog or a toad than have been

made a man. I reckoned that the most defiled creature . . . was a better thing than myself, for I had sinned against Almighty God."

He attended services at first one church and then another, hoping he might hear something that would help remove his burden. "One man preached Divine sovereignty," he says, "but what was that sublime truth to a poor sinner who wished to know what he must do to be saved. There was another admirable man who always preached about the law, but what was the use of ploughing up ground that needed to be sown. Another was a practical preacher . . . but it was very much like a commanding officer teaching maneuvers of war to a set of men without feet. . . . What I wanted to know was 'How can I get my sins forgiven?' and they never told me that."[5]

There comes a time in our lives when we want to know God's forgiveness. Human experience, as people doing wrong and being wronged, leads us to this place. We want to know it as a heartfelt experience, as we sense the release of shame and guilt; and we want to know it intellectually, meaning something our mind can see and rejoice in. We want to know that it's based on a higher authority than our own opinion, and we want to know how we ought to live in light of the experience.

GOD'S WINSOME INVITATION

Long before we started asking questions about God's forgiveness, God sent us a bold and sweet invitation to seek it. He says in Isaiah 1:18,

> "Come now, let us reason together,"
>   says the LORD.
> "Though your sins are like scarlet,
>   they shall be as white as snow;
> though they are red as crimson,
>   they shall be like wool."

What an amazing invitation: "Come now, let us reason together." He wants to reason with us. He's anticipated our questions concerning our guilt, His justice, His love, and our desire to be happy. He's ready to sit down with us and unfold everything needed to bring us into a glad sense of His forgiveness and an intimate, loving, long-term relationship with Him. "Come," He says, "I'll walk you through the experience from guilt to gladness." This winsome invitation is followed by a bold promise: "You will experience My forgiveness, and it will be great! No matter how deeply your sins have stained you with blood-red guilt, you will be washed and blanketed like freshly fallen snow with My mercy." How can God say this? Because He is the one that is going to do the cleansing and transforming work. That is His promise.

Faith in God's promise, therefore, is the starting point in the journey from guilt to gladness. This faith can be weak and full of fears and unanswered questions to begin with. But it must have two qualities. It must believe that God exists and that God is good. This we must believe or we'll get nowhere. Hebrews 11:6 says, "Without faith it is impossible to please God, because anyone who comes to Him must believe that He exists and that He rewards those who earnestly seek Him."

While this might seem so simple as to be not worth mentioning, I have learned otherwise. Trust in God, from our first consideration of Him till our last breath, has many enemies. In truth, the real battle we face in moving from guilt to gladness is against unbelief. God promises something and we believe it's too good to be true. God warns and we don't believe He is serious. God woos and we don't believe He's talking to us. God instructs but our own understanding of the way things ought to be seems oh-so-much better. God unsheathes His wrath and we think He is bluffing. That's unbelief. Worse, it's calling God a liar.

If God doesn't exist, we will of course not seek His (nonexisting) love and mercy. If we believe He does exist but that He's too busy or not interested in us, or has nothing good to offer us, or has no power to help us, then we'll not bother to seek Him either. Since every journey begins with a starting point, ours must be this: faith in a great and good God, and His great and good promises.

If this is our beginning, then our journey will end gladly. That, too, is His promise. Jeremiah 31:13-14,33-34 says,

"Maidens will dance and be glad,
young men and old as well.
I will turn their mourning into gladness;
I will give them comfort and joy instead of sorrow. . . .
This is the covenant I will make . . . ,"
declares the LORD,
"I will put my law in their minds
and write it on their hearts.
I will be their God,
and they will be my people. . . .
For I will forgive their wickedness
and will remember their sins no more."

Isn't the future fulfillment of this promise worth going after? It means taking time to understand the message of the gospel and to grasp its implications to a greater degree than we've ever done before. But the end ought to fuel the beginning. The journey will be worth it.

A MATTER OF FIRST IMPORTANCE

The apostle Paul says the journey from guilt to gladness is not only worth it, it's a matter of first importance. In 1 Corinthians 15:1-3 he writes,

I want to remind you of the gospel I preached to you, which you received and on which you have taken your stand. By this gospel you are saved, if you hold firmly to the word I preached to you. Otherwise you have believed in vain.

For what I received I passed on to you as of *first* importance: that Christ died for our sins.

28

Paul is summarizing the essence of the Christian faith. It boils down to this, he says: Christ died for our sins. These are simple words, but they convey deep truths. The gospel is far from trite. Most people don't understand these words in any life-changing way, and Paul recognized that. In their shallow, truncated, oversimplified, and easily swayed confession, Paul says, they have "believed in vain" (15:2).

I take this to mean that in terms of making a difference in one's life, one's belief in the gospel can be so shallow and unaffecting that it's no different than outright unbelief in the gospel. Such people may believe, matter-of-factly, that Christ died for their sins—they may recite the creed, sing it in a hymn, tell others the truth of it—but it's merely dogma, stuck between the ears. It's lifeless truth. And lifeless truth is of no more value than outright disbelief in the truth. That is what it means to believe in vain.

Alice very nearly fits this description. Alice had been good all her life. Her sense of sin was all in her head. She had no real sense of being saved from anything, only that she was "saved." In Alice's heart, she really believed she was a pretty good person who pleased herself, her parents, and her God. She suffered from a shallow view of her sinfulness and personal guilt and thus had a shallow appreciation of God's forgiveness. Once she stepped off the ledge of sexual purity, her conscience condemned her without mercy. She was convinced that her end was destruction.

Did Alice have a weak faith or a vain faith? Was she a Christian who fell? Or was she a nonChristian because until now her conscience has never been awakened to anything in her life that made her dependent on Christ for forgiveness? I don't know. Either way the solution is the same. Tasting the bitterness of sin, shame, and guilt, she needed to get hold of God's forgiveness as a heartfelt experience. I suggested to Alice that perhaps she had not so much lost her salvation but was for the first time discovering why she really needed a Savior. "Alice," I said. "There is a reason the gospel is called 'good news of great joy.'" Then she cried some more, but they were tears of a very different sort. They sprang from the wellspring of gladness, not despair.

That Christ died for our *sins* affirms the reality of human guilt. That Christ *died* for our sins affirms the reality of the wrath of a holy God against sinners like Alice, Antoinette and Rich, Eva and her father, and you and me. As Paul said, "The wages of sin is death" (Romans 6:23). That it was *Christ* who died for our sins affirms the love of God for sinners and His sincere desire to bring us from guilt to gladness. This is essentially the aim of this book: to unfold the true guilt of all mankind, the awesome gift of God's forgiveness offered in Christ Jesus, and the gladness of heart that takes root and grows from holding firm to the forgiveness of God like a poor man clinging to a winning lottery ticket.

A STORY OF HEARTFELT FORGIVENESS

History is richly studded with brilliant testimonies affirming that God has given many people, great and small, a heartfelt experience of His forgiveness. King David's experience is one. For Michelangelo, David was the archetypal man. His statue of David is ruggedly strong and handsome; David is presented as courageous, visionary, manly in form and temperament. King David was also a godly man—a man after God's own heart, says the Scripture. But David was also a sinful man, and as such, a guilty man, as much in need of God's forgiveness as any that will read this book.

In one period of his life, when he was feeling strong about his kingdom and perhaps arrogant about his success in politics and war, David grew weak in his relationship with God. Henri Nouwen quotes the rabbinical proverb, "He who thinks that he is finished is finished."[6] Paul said it this way in 1 Corinthians 10:12: "So if you think you are standing firm, be careful that you don't fall!" This was David's condition. It was in the spring when armies were engaged in battles and kings accompanied them to oversee the conflict. But this spring King David was at home. Already in the wrong place, he was vulnerable.

David broke what I call the three-second rule. Most men I know, including myself, are painfully aware how the sight of a woman can incite our lustful fallen nature. While I cannot always prevent seeing a suggestive picture, I know that I have about three seconds to decide whether to turn my eye and keep a pure heart or linger on and feed the spirit of lust.

The story goes that David was on the roof of his house, killing time, when he spotted Bathsheba bathing nude across the way. David lingered long past the three-second mark. He lusted after her though she was married to a soldier who was at that moment risking his life in battle for King David and Israel.

David used his great name and position to seduce Bathsheba. She got pregnant and David panicked. Instead of confessing his sexual immorality, he tried to hide it. Since abortion was not available, he did the next best thing. He called Bathsheba's husband, Uriah, home from the battlefield under the guise of needing a war report and invited him to go home to his wife before returning to battle.

David's plan, of course, was that Uriah would sleep with his wife and, subsequently, be deceived into thinking that Bathsheba's baby was theirs. But Uriah was a faithful man, and he believed that the demands of faithfulness in that instance meant not enjoying the pleasures of marital intimacy when his brothers were away from their families, fighting and dying. He slept on the palace porch that night, probably knowing that if he saw his wife for three seconds he might think again. The Scripture says she was a very beautiful woman (2 Samuel 11:2).

King David delayed Uriah's return to battle another night and insisted he eat and drink with him. He got Uriah drunk in an effort to loosen the moral resolve of this godly husband and soldier. That too failed. So David rewarded Uriah's deep devotion to God and the king by murdering him. He sent Uriah back to battle, with a note for his general that read, "Put Uriah in the front line where the fighting is fiercest. Then withdraw from him so he will be struck down and die" (2 Samuel 11:15).

Is this not despicably evil? David, just by being home rather than with his army, is guilty of abandoning his responsibility as commander in chief. That by itself is no small sin, as any soldier will tell you. But to this sin we may add the sin of lust and the abuse of power (when the king calls you, you don't refuse). David here commits the sin of sexual immorality and then begins to deceive and manipulate. He begins living a lie. David is guilty of betraying a soldier's devotion. He, like Judas, betrayed him unto death under the guise of friendship. Judas betrayed a King with a kiss. Here the king betrayed a follower with a smile and a note. This is far more evil than I can adequately describe.

To all this we may add that David lived, after the murder of Uriah, like nothing was wrong. He took Bathsheba into his house as a wife and pretended that everything was hunky-dory. He was living in denial of his sin and guilt, as we all do. But God exposed it, as He always does in due time. Nathan the prophet was sent to confront King David with these words:

> This is what the LORD, the God of Israel, says: "I anointed you king over Israel . . . [and] I gave you the house of Israel and Judah. And if all this had been too little, I would have given you even more. Why did you despise the word of the LORD by doing what is evil in His eyes? You struck down Uriah the Hittite with the sword and took his wife to be your own. You killed him with the sword of the Ammonites. Now, therefore, the sword will never depart from your house, because you despised me and took the wife of Uriah the Hittite to be your own." (2 Samuel 12:7-10)

David's denial broke: "I have sinned against the LORD" (12:13). David wept and fasted before the Lord (12:21). Never again did he deny the exceeding sinfulness of his sin or question the justness of God's punishment. In Psalm 51, David pours out his confession,

> I know my transgressions,
>   and my sin is always before me.
> Against you, you only, have I sinned
>   and done what is evil in your sight,

> so that you are proved right when you speak
> and justified when you judge. (verses 3-4)

God did judge him severely and openly for his sin. Nathan spoke for the Lord: "Out of your own household I am going to bring calamity upon you. Before your very eyes I will take your wives and give them to one who is close to you, and he will lie with your wives in broad daylight. You did it in secret, but I will do this thing in broad daylight before all Israel" (2 Samuel 12:11-12).

In the subsequent years of his life, David witnessed sexual immorality, betrayal, murder, and death among his own family members, just as he had done these things secretly against the household of Israel (2 Samuel 11–21). But, although there were serious and painful consequences for David's sin, as there is with ours, Nathan reassured David, "The LORD has taken away your sin. You are not going to die" (12:13).

I tell this long story in order to make the point that no matter how far in sin we have gone, no matter how vile our sin, no matter how permanent and unrepairable the damage to ourselves and others caused by our sin, David is proof that we can move experientially from guilt to gladness through the forgiveness of God.

In Psalm 51 David thirsts for a heartfelt experience of God's forgiveness:

> Have mercy on me, O God,
>   according to your unfailing love;
> according to your great compassion
>   blot out my transgressions.
> Wash away all my iniquity
>   and cleanse me from my sin. (verses 1-2)

David asked God to cleanse his guilty conscience:

> Cleanse me with hyssop, and I will be clean;
>   wash me, and I will be whiter than snow. (verse 7)

David was gladdened at the thought of receiving God's forgiveness:

> Let me hear joy and gladness;
>> let the bones you have crushed rejoice.
> Hide your face from my sins
>> and blot out all my iniquity. (verses 8-9)

David resolved to live confidently in his restored relationship
to God and serve Him energetically:

> Restore to me the joy of your salvation
>> and grant me a willing spirit, to sustain me.
> Then I will teach transgressors your ways,
>> and sinners will turn back to you. (verses 12-13)

David moved from guilt before God to gladness in God:

> Praise the LORD, O my soul,
>> and forget not all His benefits—
> who *forgives* all your sins
>> and heals all your diseases,
> who redeems your life from the pit
>> and crowns you with love and compassion,
> who satisfies your desires with good things
>> so that your youth is renewed like the eagle's.
>> (Psalm 103:2-5)

David experienced the anguish of guilt. But he made the
journey and, like a soaring eagle, is free to worship God. This
is where we want to go. As Martin Luther said, "Where there is
forgiveness of sins there is life and blessedness." David's experience taught him the same thing.

> Blessed is he
>> whose transgressions are forgiven,
>> whose sins are covered.
> Blessed is the man

> whose sin the LORD does not count against him
> and in whose spirit is no deceit.
> (Psalm 32:1-2)

Blessed means happy; not the temporary, low-voltage happiness that comes from yucking it up at the basketball game with friends and a few beers. That kind of happiness, like cheap batteries, burns out quickly. Blessedness is a deep, abiding happiness in God. Blessed (glad of heart) are all those who experience a heartfelt encounter with the forgiveness of God. The shame is lifted. The gnashing of teeth stops. Guilt gives way to gladness. Always has. Always will. From kings to clerks to computer nerds to poets, men and women alike can all testify to the transformation from guilt to gladness.

And what of Alice, Rich and Antoinette, Eva, and myself? Whether Alice was a Christian who fell into sin or a nonChristian merely coming to know her true need of Christ, I can't tell. It doesn't matter. What matters is that she believed on the promises of God that He desired to forgive her and bring her into a glad relationship with Himself. Thankfully, Alice was never pregnant. The last time I talked to Alice, she told me how much sweeter her relationship to God is and how much more grace she has for the weaknesses and failures of others now.

Rich and Antoinette made a commitment to keep their baby and did. We secured Rich a job with a painting company. Two months after the baby was born, I took them through counseling and conducted their wedding. They're in the process of learning the true nature of God, and just awakening to how much they need His forgiveness.

Eva is healing from her many wounds. She's learned to forgive her father. He, in turn, is now drug and alcohol free. Recently Eva wrote that she has established a close relationship with her father. He's felt deep shame about what he did to Eva. Perhaps he now feels that his deeds are unforgivable. Perhaps one day he'll get hold of the forgiveness of God, too.

And me? Though I have been a Christian for nearly twenty-five years, I am drawn to know more fully the gospel that has so changed my life. Sometimes I am driven to know by sheer joy. Other times by a sense of my own continuing need for forgiveness. "Come now, let us *reason* together," said the Lord. By these words we are all invited to search out the forgiveness of God in Scripture, reasoning out His Word and moving experientially along the path from guilt to gladness.

∽

The Journey from Guilt to Gladness

Our starting point in the journey toward gladness is faith that God exists and that He rewards those who, trusting in His promises, seek Him diligently.

Part One
Our Guilt

Chapter Two

Forgiveness Desired

OWNING UP TO OUR GUILT

*God touches the spring of penitence in men through many deep experiences,
but the experience is always that of beholding a goodness that shames us.*
—H. R. MACKINTOSH, *THE CHRISTIAN EXPERIENCE OF FORGIVENESS*

☙

*Once you were alienated from God and were enemies
in your minds because of your evil behavior.*
—COLOSSIANS 1:21

The first-century biographer Plutarch said, "Medicine, to produce health, has to examine disease; and music, to create
harmony, must investigate discord."[1] So the first step from guilt
to gladness is painful. God, the surgeon of our souls, makes a
deep cut into our natural pride with a sharp truth. That truth is
this: We feel guilty because we *are* guilty. I can't say it more
plainly than that. For many that is too plain.

By nature we tend to be open to a variety of possible ori-
gins for guilt, but not so open to this one. We're open to the
suggestion that a person's guilt originates in an overly harsh
parental upbringing. Or that guilt stems from the old nuns in
their stealth-winged hats; they *make* people feel guilty. Less religion leads to less guilt, some specialists tell us. Perhaps our guilt
is due to our "inner child" not being affirmed enough when our
entire body was less than four feet tall. Maybe guilt originates
from a chemical imbalance in the brain. Maybe it is just a delu-
sion: we're hearing voices that aren't real. Maybe it springs from
low self-esteem and we need to reprogram ourselves—stand in

front of the mirror like comic Stuart Smally and say, "I'm good enough, I'm smart enough, and doggone it, people like me!" We laugh, but maybe guilt comes from a sick perfectionism. A bubbling brew of all these explanations might explain the origin of our guilt.

Naturally, it's tempting to believe any explanation about our guilt that ends with the sentence, "So, my friend, there is no *justifiable* reason for you to feel guilty — it's not *your* fault." Plenty of books will tell us this, as will plenty of religious swamis. Plenty of therapists are willing to sift through our memories until they find the clinker that set off our guilt, so we can remove it. People spend thousands of dollars to confirm that the origin of their guilt is found in what somebody else did to wound them. We may feel hurt because we are wounded, but we feel guilty because we *are* guilty.

GETTING HONEST ABOUT OUR GUILT

The hardest thing in life is acknowledging personal guilt. For me, it's harder than admitting I'm sick. I refuse to believe it; I ignore the signs; I deny the pain. And the cure goes unsought. In the same way, until we own up to the truth that we feel guilty because we are guilty, God's forgiveness will remain unsought and unfound. Jesus put it this way: "It is not the healthy who need a doctor, but the sick. I have not come to call the righteous, but sinners to repentance" (Luke 5:31-32). Only when I realize my guilt will I sense my need for God's forgiveness and start desiring it.

Our natural belief about ourselves is that we're pretty darn good people, though we're not too proud to admit we've made a few "mistakes" along the way. This allows us to confess a little guilt, but in a self-flattering way. Another way we do this is to say, "Well, I admit I'm not *perfect*." When my wife makes some admiring comment about me, I've never thought of replying, "Now, honey, remember, I'm not perfect." But I have been tempted to say it whenever anyone has pressed me to admit to something I've done wrong. "Hey, I'm not perfect." Translation:

"Other than a blemish or two, I sparkle, so get off my case!" Other people like the phrase "I'm only human." This really means "my sin should be excused because as a human being I really can't help it."

Even when we own up to our guilt, we usually attempt to shift attention to our woundedness and away from our waywardness. We pray, "Forgive me, because I only sinned a little, and I only did it once, and only because so-and-so did such-and-such to me." This is a clever way of admitting to guilt while justifying it at the same time. Another way we put the best spin on guilt is to say, "God, forgive me. I really didn't mean it." In other words, we meant well. Our hearts were *good*. This prayer for forgiveness is based on our really *not* needing it. It's really a cry to be understood, not forgiven.

It's stunning, then, to read how King David prayed.

> For Thy name's sake, O LORD,
> Pardon my iniquity, for it is great. (Psalm 25:11, NASB)

What a radical prayer! David prays in the exact opposite direction of most people. What is prayed for? God's forgiveness. What needs to be forgiven? My *iniquity*, not my infirmities. Whose sin? *My very own*. Why should God forgive me? Because it's just a little sin? No, because my iniquity is *very great*! And why should God forgive great sinners like me? So that the greatness of God's mercy might become famous— "for Thy name's sake, O LORD."

Compare David's way of handling his personal guilt with that of my friend Bob. Bob is a devout man who goes to Mass regularly. He reads the Bible. He's a helpful neighbor. He works hard and loves his wife. He's helped me out in finding resources for young pregnant moms, delivering cribs and maternity clothes. But beneath Bob's devotion and concern for others is an intensely angry man immersed in guilt.

He has reasons to be angry, and he has reasons to be guilty. Bob was severely mistreated by his father as a child. It's the divine duty of every father to nurture sons and train them to be honorable men, so it's easy to understand why a boy would grow up angry when he suffers injustice upon injustice from his own father. Add to this the reality that life itself is unfair, and one searching for reasons to be angry will surely find them.

One day, many years ago, Bob was driving down the road with his first wife. Something she said or did triggered Bob's anger. He was so angry he started driving faster and faster. As a result, Bob lost control of his car and crashed it. Tragically, his wife was mortally wounded. Though rushed to the hospital, she died after a few days. Adding to Bob's pain, he had to authorize the removal of a respirator that was keeping her breathing even though she had no brain waves. She was only twenty-one.

"I murdered my wife," he told me. "I can never forgive myself."

I might say, "But you did not *intend* to kill her. What happened was an accident; a murder is when you intentionally kill someone." But Bob is not remembering the horror of mangled steel and shattered glass and blood as a lawyer! His heart is broken and he's overwhelmed with regret. While it's probably true that he's being too hard on himself, he is surely culpable to *some* degree. Bob's conscience is not lying, even if it's overstating the situation. It seems both wrong and foolish to try to convince Bob that his guilt has no basis in reality. In a thousand years, with a billion dollars worth of psychiatric care, I do not believe Bob could find relief. Bob's temper was sinful, his driving reckless, and the death of his wife preventable. The guilt he feels is justified and reality-based.

THE BIBLICAL EXPLANATION OF THE ORIGIN OF GUILT

A good place to begin understanding the true reality of guilt and its consequences is Colossians 1:21: "Once you were alienated from God and were enemies in your minds *because of your evil behavior.*" The guilt and self-condemnation that play like a never-ending cassette tape in our minds originate from what we did — our evil behavior. Not what our parents did. Not what society did. Not what God did in creating us. We feel guilty because we *know* that what we did was evil, even damnable. Bob's guilt over the exceeding sinfulness of his temper is precisely as it should be, according to Colossians 1:21. He feels guilty because his behavior was evil. He may feel hurt from wounds suffered in childhood and life in general, but his temper tantrum was evil, and it got his wife killed.

Colossians 1:21 says we feel guilty because we are guilty of doing evil. But it says more. It teaches us that our evil behavior has alienated us from a righteous God: "Once you were *alienated* from God and were *enemies* in your minds because of your evil behavior." It isn't that we don't believe that God is good and loving. We do. It's that we feel alienated from God's goodness and love because of what we've done. It's not that we don't want His blessing. We would gladly receive it. It's that we feel God is justified in withholding it. On this we should trust our feelings. For the painful truth is, we *feel* alienated from God because we *are* alienated from God. Isaiah 59:1-3,12,14 says,

> Surely the arm of the LORD is not too short to save,
> nor His ear too dull to hear.
> But your iniquities have *separated*
> you from your God;
> your sins have *hidden His face* from you,
> so that He will not hear.
> For your hands are stained with blood,
> your fingers with guilt.
> Your lips have spoken lies,
> and your tongue mutters wicked things. . . .
> For our offenses are many in your sight,
> and our sins testify against us. . . .
> So justice is *driven back,*
> and *righteousness stands at a distance.*

Our sin separates us from God. The reality of this alienation is not only confirmed in Scripture but our own conscience bears witness to it. Colossians 1:21 says, "You were . . . enemies in your minds because of your evil behavior." *In our own minds* we sense God's righteous displeasure and His judgment against us. The experience of guilt, then, is the videotape replay of our own evil behavior in the pretrial hearings that are held long before that final day of judgment. This pretrial hearing room is called the conscience.

THE GUILTY CONSCIENCE

The Bible doesn't tell us where the conscience is, and searching for it would be "like groping for a black cat in a dark room where no black cat has ever been." Instead, the Bible uses a variety of metaphors to describe the workings of our conscience. Colossians 1:21 points to the reflective capacity of our conscience: we have become enemies with God *in our minds*. In Matthew 5:8 the conscience is referred to as the *heart*: "Blessed are the pure in heart." The conscience can feel as well as think. Hebrews 10:22 uses the word *heart* together with *conscience*. We need to have our "hearts sprinkled to cleanse us from a guilty conscience." Even heart and mind are not simple categories for feelings and thought. In Ephesians 1:18 the apostle Paul prays that "the eyes of your heart may be enlightened." The point is not *where* the conscience is, but *what* is its function.

O. Hallesby was one of Norway's leading Christian teachers. He played a leading role in the church's opposition to the Nazis and was confined to a concentration camp for two years. He knows something about conscience. He wrote, "The conscience is the simplest and clearest expression of the exalted character and dignity of human life. Here we touch upon something which makes man a man and exalts him above the animals."[2] Animals live by instinct. They do what they do without guilt or remorse. A dog may put his tail between his legs when he's caught digging in the trash can, but a dog is not burdened by a guilty conscience. He may fear a scolding or regret that he got caught before he could reach the chicken bones, but he doesn't lie in his bed thinking, *Why did I do that? I know I'm not supposed to. I'm so ashamed. I wonder if my father snooped in the trash.* We're unique among creation; we're endowed with a conscience by our Creator.

The conscience is that faculty by which we know, together with God, whether we are living in conformity to His good and perfect will for our lives. God's good and perfect will is expressed in His moral law. "Just as He who called you is holy, so be holy in all you do; for it is written: 'Be holy, because I am holy'" (1 Peter 1:15-16; cf. Leviticus 11:44). This moral law is imprinted on everyone's conscience. Everyone's conscience bears witness that God is holy and righteous, and that it's right to love such a God and be like Him. It speaks unequivocally that it's wicked to ignore such a great God and go our own way. Therefore the conscience is an objective witness of our relationship to God.

The ancient Greek dramatist Menander (342-292 B.C.) said, "Conscience is a god to all mortals." Romans 2:14-15 confirms this.

> When Gentiles, who do not have the law, do by nature things required by the law, they are a law for themselves, even though they do not have the law, since they show that the requirements of the law are written on their hearts, their consciences also bearing witness, and their thoughts now accusing, now even defending them.

Through the conscience we sense the moral will of God and know something about our own conformity or conflict with it. It's important to note that this knowledge is shared. We know it *together with God.* Through my conscience I sense not only right and wrong but God's pleasure or displeasure as well. When I lie, I know I've done wrong. I also know that God knows I lied. I also know that He agrees with my conscience that I've done wrong. And I know that God knows that I know I've done wrong.

Thus there begins a straining of relationship between God and me. My sinful behavior is registered in my conscience as guilt before God and causes us both to withdraw from each other. I withdraw because I sense the reality of my sinfulness and, in light of His righteousness, I fear God's judgment. God withdraws out of faithfulness to His own righteousness. As Isaiah said, "Righteousness stands at a distance" (Isaiah 59:14).

YOU'RE HURTING MY SELF-ESTEEM

The dominant social theory of the day says that self-worth, self-respect, and self-esteem are the cure for antisocial behavior. Guilt poisons a person's ability to feel good about himself. Therefore, feeling guilty is bad. As a resident of Boston's inner city, I see plenty of social decay every day. Every week I read how kids commit crimes and take drugs, and I'm told it's because they have no respect for themselves. "Teach them self-respect and they won't take drugs and rob people." This is axiomatic among social workers, educators, community activists, and youth workers.

Young people know that people putting everything into the self-esteem basket can be played for fools. It allows everyone to pretend there is no innate desire in us to do wrong. It allows us to deny that there is a gut-level pleasure in certain immoral and destructive behavior. But the reality of the streets is that taking drugs feels good to them, and "them" is the central person they care about. They love self, value self, and esteem self above all others. People deal drugs not because they have low self-esteem, but because the big money it brings in means they can buy some sleek wheels and fine clothes and be a *somebody*. A drug dealer's sense of self-worth is so high that he thinks he deserves to be a *somebody* in everyone else's eyes as well as in his own.

I recognize there is a sense of worthlessness that affects some people that is entirely unhealthy and unbiblical. Such a person believes other people are valuable but he is not. The fact that we are made in the image of God places a value on us not found in any other creature. Jesus said, "How much more valuable you are than birds!" (Luke 12:24). It's tragic when a child is cursed from childhood and told he is worthless as a worm. This is a despicable lie. The problem with self-loathing, however, is that it's still an expression of self-centeredness. The cure will not come by exchanging one kind of self-centeredness for another.

In comparison, God called Israel a worm (Isaiah 41:14). But here the contrast is between our helplessness and God's helpfulness. Apart from God and His redeeming grace, we would be as helpless as a worm. We certainly would be no better than a

46

worm apart from God's unique imprint on us as humans. In a similar context, Paul called himself a wretched man (Romans 7:24). He considered the glory and majesty of God and saw His exceeding sinfulness in not loving so great a God wholeheartedly. But he felt as helpless as a worm to change, and he looked to God for help. This is good.

John Newton wrote the famous hymn "Amazing Grace:"

> Amazing grace! How sweet the sound, that saved a wretch like me!
> I once was lost but now I'm found, was blind but now I see.

Newton was not suffering from low self-esteem when he called himself a wretch. He was drunk with the grandeur of God's love.

Isaac Watts wrote another of the church's favorite hymns, "Alas! And Did My Savior Bleed!"

> Alas! And did my Savior bleed? And did my Sovereign die?
> Would He devote that sacred head for such a worm as I?[3]

In calling himself a worm, Watts is saying that he knows himself to be a guilty sinner; one given over to sin. He's acknowledging that there is no moral goodness *in himself* that motivated Christ's death on our behalf.

But someone may object, "God loves me. Christ died for me. Therefore I must be really valuable to God since He paid so high a price for me." Indeed, it's more common than not to hear the cross of Christ proclaimed in this self-esteem–inflating way. But Romans 5:8 says something very different. "God demonstrates His own love for us in this: While we were still sinners, Christ died for us." It's true that God's love compelled Him to send His Son into the world to die for our sins (see also John 3:16). It's *not* true that His love for us, expressed in the Cross, is motivated chiefly by our inherent value and goodness. Christ's death for us is chiefly motivated by the value He places on *Himself* and His own glory as a loving God. He desires to display His love as the glorious thing it is before all creation, that we might be impressed with His value, not our own. To accomplish this, He displays a love so awesome and far-reaching that it can love the unlovely. Paul would never say, "The fact that Jesus died for me shows me how valuable I am to God." Instead, he was amazed because he saw himself as the "worst of sinners." In 1 Timothy 1:15-16 he wrote,

> Here is a trustworthy saying that deserves full acceptance: Christ Jesus came into the world to save sinners—of whom I am the worst. But for that very reason I was shown mercy so that in me, the worst of sinners, Christ Jesus might display His unlimited patience as an example for those who would believe on Him and receive eternal life.

According to Paul, it wasn't something in himself that motivated Christ's sacrifice, it was something in God. What was it? "I was shown mercy *so that* in me . . . Christ Jesus might display *His unlimited patience.*" Paul saw that God's forgiveness highlighted the excellency of God's patience, not his own goodness or worth. God loves us as guilty sinners, not as *somebodies.* When a worm is loved, he rejoices in the wonder of such love. When a princess is loved, she's apt to think it her due.

THE PRINCESS WHO THOUGHT SHE WAS *SOMEBODY*

George MacDonald wrote "The Wise Woman or the Lost Princess," a wonderful children's story that illustrates that when it comes to self, more is worse, and less is best:

> A baby girl was born; and her father was a king and her mother was a queen. . . . So the little girl was a Somebody. As she grew up, everybody about her did his best to convince her that she was Somebody; and the girl herself was so easily persuaded of it that she quite forgot that anybody had ever told her so, and took it for a fundamental, innate, primary, first-born, self-evident, necessary, and incontrovertible idea and principle that she was

Somebody. And far be it from me to deny it. I will even go so far as to assert that in this odd country there was a huge number of Somebodies; and the worst of it was that the princess never thought of there being more than one Somebody—and that was herself.[4]

The story goes on to describe how the princess's self-love leads to terrible behavior—she throws tantrums and mistreats others. All evil behavior is motivated by an overinflated sense of self-worth that supplants the worth of God and the worth of others. That is written into the genetic code of every sinful action: me first, me last, glory be to me. Frederick Buechner said it well, "We all tend to make ourselves the center of the universe."[5]

We live in a world where everybody looks to everybody else to make himself or herself happy. To paraphrase Christian psychologist Larry Crabb, everybody's a tick in search of a dog![6] This is our problem. In searching for God's forgiveness, we must not pin our hopes on God finding us so valuable that He feels compelled to forgive us. We must pin our hopes on God wanting to show us the value of His love for guilty sinners.

IF I STEAL, AM I A THIEF?

When we break the moral law of God, we become lawbreakers. Doing evil makes us evildoers. When I sin, I confirm that I am by nature a sinner. When I was a young teenager, I stole a hat from a store. I did not lack self-esteem. I lacked a hat that I wanted. What's worse, I arrived at the store with a wad of money in my pocket from a newspaper job I had. Staring at the price tag, I thought, *Hey, why should I spend my money, money I worked so hard to get, on that hat? I can get it for nothing by pinching it, then save my money for something else.* I even esteemed my own keen insight at that moment!

As I headed for the door, the store manager stopped me. I turned six shades of green and wished I was dead. The manager saw I was not yet a hardened criminal and sent me home with instructions to have my parents call him back with the news or he would call the police. I went home to take my lumps. To this day, I remember what my eighteen-year-old sister said when she overheard me confessing. With disgust dripping from her voice she said, "How totally embarrassing. I've got a brother who's a thief!"

She called me a thief! Clearly she didn't know that this could make me worse, by damaging my self-image. Shouldn't she have tried to build up my self-esteem by saying, "You know, you're really a great kid, and I'm so glad you're my brother. You're a very special person, and stealing is beneath you"? She said in effect, "You're nothing but a stupid sinner, and you should be ashamed of yourself."

Becoming ashamed of what we are as a result of what we do is a good and necessary part of getting real about guilt. If you murder, you become a murderer. If you commit adultery, you are an adulterer. If you lie, you become a liar. If you steal, you are a thief, not "a person of low self-esteem." I stole, and I had become a thief. It led me to my room weeping and ashamed of myself. But that was good! Painful, but good.

MY NAME IS LEGION

The reality is, all of us have sinned and are guilty before God. You may have done some things I have not and vice versa, but in the end we are partners in crime in need of pardon. C. S. Lewis was an English scholar and a resolved atheist for many years prior to becoming a celebrated Christian apologist and writer. He wanted to be an atheist because he wanted to keep his independence. He called God the *Interferer*. But to justify his independence from God, he felt "an attempt at complete virtue must be made" (then he wouldn't need God or His forgiveness). Of this effort he wrote:

> Really, a young atheist cannot guard his faith too carefully.
> Dangers lie in wait for him on every side. You must not
> do, you must not even try to do the will of the Father

unless you are prepared to "know the doctrine." All my acts, desires, and thoughts were to be brought into harmony with universal Spirit. For the first time I examined myself with a seriously practical purpose. And there I found what appalled me; a zoo of lusts, a bedlam of ambitions, a nursery of fears, a harem of fondled hatreds. My name was legion.[7]

When Lewis says we must be prepared to "know the doctrine," he means that if we would enjoy the beauty of holiness we must first discover the reality of our sinful nature. "If we claim we have not sinned, we make [God] out to be a liar and His word has no place in our lives" (1 John 1:10). This is truly one of the sharpest warnings in all the Bible. It's saying that denying the reality of sin and the reality of its evilness is not itself a neutral opinion; it's an accusatory action. It accuses God of lying when He calls us guilty sinners. This makes God evil. If, then, God is evil, truly we are beyond hope. If we accuse the God of all glory of being evil, surely we will regret the day He comes to vindicate the goodness of His name.

BEHOLDING A GOODNESS THAT SHAMES US

Ultimately God shows us the reality of our guilt by showing us the purity of His goodness. H. R. Mackintosh said, "God touches the spring of penitence in men through many deep experiences, but the experience is always that of beholding a goodness that shames us."[8] God is good and everything He does reflects His goodness. "Good and upright is the LORD" (Psalm 25:8). "You [God] are good, and what you do is good" (Psalm 119:68).
Isaiah saw the goodness of the Lord.

I saw the Lord seated on a throne, high and exalted, and the train of His robe filled the temple. Above Him were seraphs, each with six wings: With two wings they covered their faces, with two they covered their feet, and with two they were flying. And they were calling to one another:

51

"Holy, holy, holy is the LORD Almighty;
the whole earth is full of His glory." (Isaiah 6:1-3)

The light of God's goodness revealed the cracks in Isaiah's character.

"Woe to me!" I cried. "I am ruined! For I am a man of unclean lips, and I live among a people of unclean lips, and my eyes have seen the King, the LORD Almighty." (6:5)

When we see the God of glory, all that will be real is the splendor of His majesty and the harsh reality of our sin. As we live now, what is real is our house payment due on the first of the month, or the fact that we haven't eaten since breakfast and it's now past eight at night. We know sex is real; we know for sure our neighbor is an idiot and our political leaders are fools. Reality is chemotherapy, car crashes, and funerals of precious family and friends. Reality is being laid off, seeing your kids move away, and being fitted for a hearing aid. That's all real. But sin and guilt? Pardon or punishment? How real is that? Doesn't God understand why I do what I do? Can't He cut me some slack? But when we stand before the God of glory, all that will be real is death or pardon at the hand of so great a God. All that was once so real, so certain, will seem a Chimera. Before Him the truth of ourselves is laid bare and there will be no thought of denial, rationalization, blame, or bribery. Our guilt will never seem so real as at that moment.

THE MOUSE'S SEARCH FOR THE CAT

Ask a hundred people if they want forgiveness, and a hundred people will say, "Yeah, sure, and can I have fries with that and a large Pepsi?" They have no great sense of needing God's forgiveness but believe it wouldn't hurt to have it in their pocket just in case. Religion is, I fear, most often practiced to buy off God's anger, to pay for a sin done, so that one is free to go on in it. We throw ourselves into church or confession like a burglar might throw a steak to a watchdog—to keep him at a safe distance. Still others sense the reality of their guilt but want to come up with their own creative (and always less painful) method of obtaining God's pardon. They invent new religions to avoid the painful truth about personal guilt before the God of infinite glory.

"I had rather," Charles Spurgeon wrote, "pass through seven years of the most languishing sickness, than I would ever again pass through the terrible discovery of the evil of sin."9 C. S. Lewis had his own witty way of describing the inner struggle: "Amiable agnostics will talk cheerfully about 'man's search for God.' To me, as I then was, they might as well have talked about the mouse's search for the cat."10

Could anything be more out of step with the times than admitting that our deepest problem is not our woundedness but our waywardness? In an age when we get to create new realities like cyberspace, do we want to admit to the old realities of *guilt* and *sin* and *judgment* and, worst of all, *repentance?* It's far more thrilling to throw our hands out wide, like Frank Sinatra, and sing, "I did it my way." The whole world cheers then.

However, when we are tired of believing lies; when we are weary of our trite rationalizations; when we no longer want to snap, for the umpteenth time, "Shut up!" to our conscience; when trying to appease God through religion has run its course; when we no longer wish to be at war with God in our minds, what we really want is God's forgiveness. We want to see the goodness of God and experience it. We want to say with Job, "Though He slay me, yet will I hope in Him" (Job 13:15). We are ready to risk all embarrassment, all humiliation, all the pain that comes in owning up to our real guilt.

At that moment we will take a clear and certain step. We will do two things: First, we will *agree with our accusers.* Jesus advised us to "settle matters quickly with [our] adversary" (Matthew 5:25). Our conscience accuses us of sinful behavior; it blames us for doing evil and becoming evil. We agree with our accuser. Our conscience charges us with defying the moral law of God and living as an enemy of God. We agree with our accuser. The Word of God incriminates us more clearly, laying out before our eyes those things that make us guilty. It indicts us for being self-seeking, rejecting the truth, and following evil (Romans 2:8). We agree with our accuser. God charges us of breaking faith with Him, though He is good and rightly to be praised. We agree with our accuser. The Scripture reveals that our waywardness is far more serious than our woundedness. We agree.

Because we now agree that we feel guilty because we are guilty, we will also *agree with God in prayer.* Daniel's prayer is an example of the kind of confession we need to bring to God:

> I turned to the Lord God and pleaded with Him
> in prayer. . . .
> I prayed to the LORD my God and confessed:
>
> "O Lord, the great and awesome God, who keeps His covenant of love with all who love Him and obey His commands, we have sinned and done wrong. We have been wicked and have rebelled; we have turned away from your commands and laws. We have not listened to your servants. . . .
> "Lord, you are righteous, but this day we are covered with shame . . . because we have sinned against you. The Lord our God is merciful and forgiving, even though we have rebelled against Him; we have not obeyed the LORD our God or kept the laws He gave us through His servants the prophets. . . . O Lord, listen! O Lord, forgive." (Daniel 9:3-10,19)

We need to pray in the same direction King David did.

> For Thy name's sake, O LORD,
> Pardon my iniquity, for it is great. (Psalm 25:11, NASB)

In such heartfelt prayer, we have taken our first step from guilt to gladness. Do not fear to take it. C. S. Lewis laughed at his own hesitating fears in taking this step. He soon discovered that "The hardness of God is kinder than the softness of men, and His compulsion is our liberation."[11]

❦

The Journey from Guilt to Gladness

The transformation of guilt into gladness begins when we acknowledge the painful truth of our personal guilt. This means owning up to having a sinful nature and confessing our waywardness to God in prayer.

Chapter Three

Forgiveness Needed

ACKNOWLEDGING THE JUSTICE OF GOD'S JUDGMENT

*O Conscience, into what abyss of fears
And horrors hast thou driven me; out of which
I find no way, from deep to deeper plunged.*
—JOHN MILTON, *PARADISE LOST*

ॐ

*God is a righteous judge,
a God who expresses His wrath every day.*
—PSALM 7:11

Some years ago I had the joy of going to Saint Croix in the Virgin Islands with a team of twenty men and women from my church. We went to rebuild roofs for the impoverished people on the island after a devastating hurricane hit them. We worked like oil riggers but had a great time. That is not to say I didn't appreciate our day off. I went snorkeling in the bluest water I'd ever seen. Right below me in twenty feet of pristine water teemed schools of neon blue and yellow fish darting in and out of bone white castles of living coral and purple-fanned plants.

Flooded with a sense of the beauty and the glory of God as our magnificent Creator, I started slapping the surface of the water and yelling praises through my snorkel. My muffled hollering attracted the attention of the three brothers with me. At first they thought I was drowning. Soon they caught on to my joy and joined me in slapping the water and whooping it up to the praise of God above for the beauty He displayed below us. Then I swam out a little farther.

Another hundred yards out, the coral ended abruptly as the depth increased. No radiant colored fish were in sight. The rock turned barren and flat. Suddenly, and I do mean suddenly, the rock curved straight down into a gripping black abyss. Tiny candles of light shafts danced below me for some depths that I could not measure. Below that, only a dread darkness with no visible bottom.

Later I learned that I was looking at and swimming right above the island's continental shelf, which descends toward the famous Puerto Rico Trench. The ocean floor drops to 12,600 feet at this point—almost two and a half miles deep! Sharks feed along the edge. What swims at the bottom swims without eyes, for there is no light. I felt small, very small. A dread fear squeezed the air right out of my lungs. I trembled at the abyss and bolted, like a duckling seeing his first alligator, for the safety of the shoreline. As I swam past the abyss and over the beauty of the coral garden, I recalled the gripping words of Romans 11:22: "Behold . . . the kindness and severity of God" (NASB).

How can we describe God's kindness and sternness? There is mystery here beyond my wisdom. The starting point, however, is to acknowledge the reality of both of them. The God of glory is *kind*. He is also *severe*. The biblical revelation of God's severity suggests that our guilt is *deeper* than we ever knew and that our need for forgiveness is *greater* than we ever knew. Owning up to this by acknowledging the justice of God's judgment is the next step in the journey from guilt to gladness.

GETTING REAL ABOUT GOD'S WRATH

God's wrath is real. Romans 1:18 says, "The wrath of God is being revealed from heaven against all the godlessness and wickedness of men who suppress the truth by their wickedness." God reveals the reality and severity of His wrath today primarily through the hundreds of warnings and examples recorded in the Bible.[1]

The wrath of God revealed in the Bible is so terrible, so fierce, so awful, that it forces us to see and agree with God that our sin must be vastly more evil than we thought. If we resist this conclusion, we will conclude that God's punishment for sin is more severe than deserved. Our mostly hidden resentment of God's sovereign authority over us will be driven out into the open. "I could never love a God like that! I will never honor such a God. I will never feel obligated to obey and serve such a God." If we conclude that our sin is worthy of God's condemnation, we'll drop to our knees and cry out, "God, have mercy on me, a sinner" (Luke 18:13). We'll cry out like Jonah:

> From the depths of the grave I called for help,
>   and you listened to my cry. (2:2)

The revelation of God's wrath moves us closer to becoming either a God-hater or a God-glorifier. Either way, the wrath of God, as revealed in the Bible, has the effect of, as C. S. Lewis put it, "planting the flag of truth within the fortress of a rebel soul."[2]

THE JUSTICE OF GOD'S JUDGMENT

Romans 1:18-23 affirms and clarifies what our conscience, in its own way, is trying to say. It explains *what* we've done wrong, *why* it's intensely wrong, and *why* God is right to be angry with us:

> The wrath of God is being revealed from heaven against all the godlessness and wickedness of men who suppress the truth by their wickedness, since what may be known about God is plain to them, because God has made it plain to them. For since the creation of the world God's invisible qualities—His eternal power and divine nature—have been clearly seen, being understood from what has been made, so that men are without excuse.
>
> For although they knew God, they neither glorified Him as God nor gave thanks to Him, but their thinking became futile and their foolish hearts were darkened.

Although they claimed to be wise, they became fools and exchanged the glory of the immortal God for images made to look like mortal man and birds and animals and reptiles.

The apostle Paul, under the Spirit of inspiration, can sure pack a lot of truth into a few words! It's crucial that we resist the impulse to skip on by. God wants you to know these truths and follow the logic of the Spirit. To help, I've set these truths next to the questions they answer.

1. What is God's response to our sinful behavior?	Divine *wrath*.
2. What sin have we committed that deserves this judgment?	We *suppressed the truth*.
3. What truth is suppressed?	The truth of *what may be known about God*.
4. What can be known about God?	That He is an infinitely glorious and generous God.
5. What proof is there that we are suppressing this truth?	We have refused to *glorify Him as God and thank Him* for His goodness.
6. Why is this an infinitely heinous evil?	Because God has revealed the truth of His infinite glory *plainly* and *clearly* through what He has made.

The conclusion then is brought home. There is *no excuse* for not glorifying God and being thankful for His goodness toward us.

Evidently there is something so excellent, so beautiful, so majestic, so winsome about God, that not seeing it requires effort, a willful refusal to see it. "Sin is an infinite evil," wrote Robert Murray McCheyne, "because it is the breaking of an infinite obligation. Surely there are none that would say that God is not infinitely lovely; and therefore none will say that there is not an infinite obligation upon us to serve Him. Then if you and I do not do this, we are breaking an infinite obligation; and if it be an infinite evil then it demands infinite punishment."[3] We can test the truthfulness of this by checking out how visible God's glory is. The more evident God made it, the more evil it is to ignore it.

SURROUNDED BY GOD'S GLORY

The glory of God surrounds us in at least three plentiful and pleasing ways. First, it is shown clearly through all that God has made. Creation's grandeur speaks of the grandeur of the Creator. The art reflects the artist. The truth of God's glory is evident in the glory of the twinkling galaxies above, in the roar of tornadoes, in the honeybee moving from daffodil to daffodil. The goodness of God's glory is seen in seed that falls into the ground, dies, and rises up as a tree producing bushels of tangy oranges for us to enjoy. The goodness of His glory is revealed in the first cry of a newborn baby. Every created thing has its own language, but the translation is the same — "Great is the Lord and worthy to be praised!" Psalm 19:1-4 says,

> The heavens declare the glory of God;
>   the skies proclaim the work of His hands.
> Day after day they pour forth speech;
>   night after night they display knowledge.
> There is no speech or language
>   where their voice is not heard.
> Their voice goes out into all the earth,
>   their words to the ends of the world.

Second, God surrounds us with His glory by surrounding us with people.

> God created man in His own image,
>   in the image of God He created him;
>   male and female He created them. (Genesis 1:27)

61

The glory of God is uniquely imprinted into every human life to reflect back His glory and refract it for all to see. So far God has created billions of image bearers—five billion inhabit the earth at present—all designed to disseminate His glory in the world.

How do we reflect God's glory? When men and women look to God and say "Wow!" whether in praise or silent meditation, we echo God's *delight* in His own goodness. When we refrain from evil, we reflect God's *moral* glory. When we help a poor unwed mother find the resources she needs to give her baby life, we image God's *benevolent* glory. When we punish embezzlers by due process of law for stealing the life savings of hardworking families, we reflect God's *judicial* glory. As stewards over the earth we reflect His *reigning* glory. When we proclaim pardon for the guilty through Jesus Christ, we refract His *redemptive* glory.

The third way God surrounds us with His glory is through the benevolence He originally bestowed on mankind. From the moment Adam took his first breath, God demonstrated that His glory was a *benevolent glory*. Everything God made for Adam was set in place with the refrain, "And God saw that it was good" (Genesis 1:4,10,12,18). When He finished, "God saw all that He had made, and it was *very* good" (1:31).

Adam lived amidst a rich variety of God-created trees and animals. He was provided food and meaningful labor. When that was not enough, God created Eve from Adam, so that he might enjoy a level of intimacy and partnership unique to them above all the rest of creation. Together they were to live under God's benevolent rule, trusting in His goodness and enjoying His provision (Genesis 2). Everything around them echoed, "The Lord will provide!" (see Genesis 22:8).

The faith we are to place in God is a glad willingness to trust that He will provide for us everything that will truly make us happy in the long run. "Don't be deceived. . . . Every good and perfect gift is from above, coming down from the Father of the heavenly lights, who does not change like shifting shadows" (James 1:16-17). The vegetable soup, hot rolls, and butter we eat on cold winter nights can be traced to His goodness toward us. He provides work, often productive and fulfilling, though not always, to pay our phone bill. Out of His goodness come brotherly friendship, marriage, and family.

The truth that God is a *glorious* God and *worthy* to be praised is panoramically laid out in creation. It's stamped on the unique face of every coworker, neighbor, and family member we see, and it's reaffirmed every day by the benevolent provisions God makes for us. To live according to this truth would mean that we rejoice in the goodness of God and live to the praise of His glory.

DESPISING GOD'S GLORY

No one has the excuse of saying, "I didn't know that God wanted a relationship with me marked by my thankfulness for His goodness to me." We did know it; we just suppressed it. Then we went further. We replaced Him altogether with a god of our own imagination. Romans 1:23 says, "[We] exchanged the glory of the immortal God for images made to look like mortal man and birds and animals and reptiles."

This exchange from the greater to the lesser is downright foolish. It's like a man landing a job at the White House. He's appointed to serve the president in promoting the public good and sees it as the very great honor it is. He's excited to think that his service is going to advance the reputation of the president and his administration. He's a part of history. But instead of being thankful to the president and serving him gladly, suppose the man refused to acknowledge the president or form public policy "in his name." Suppose instead he foolishly started serving the White House cat and pretending she was the one in charge. Since the cat doesn't have much to say, he thinks thoughts for her. He creates a wide variety of policies he thinks the cat-president wants. All of them may clearly promote the public good. He never has to submit his judgment to the cat because, he's pleased to discover, they always agree.

While this example sounds foolhardy to the point of being humorous, bear with me a little longer. For this man everything is peachy except those brief moments when his pretense breaks down and he thinks of the day when the real president decides he has put up with the stupidity and insults and treasonous behavior long enough and must deal with this man in order to vindicate his own government. He knows the day will come. Nothing, not even the good things, the man did in the name of the cat will matter on that dreadful day. So he flushes the thought of it from his head and fetches cream and kibbles for the cat.

No matter how bizarre this sounds, it is akin to the nature of our relationship to God. He is the God of infinite glory. He has made His glory known in awesome and satisfying ways. We were made to know Him and serve Him. We rejected this service as worthless and "exchanged the glory of the immortal God for images made to look like mortal man and birds and animals and reptiles" (Romans 1:23). No wonder we're afraid to meet God one day.

Religions recast Him into a shelfload of minigods for this occasion and that. We've reshaped Him into wood and stone carvings of various zoological images. Remember the golden calf incident (Exodus 32)? God is offended by it. It's as demeaning to Him as it would be to you if someone treated you like a dog and wanted to put a leash around your neck. You would be angry, and rightly so. God declares, "I am the LORD your God[!] . . . Have no other gods before me" (Exodus 20:2-3). This includes making gods of ourselves. Claiming to be wise and beyond the myths of religion, we love, as Paul said "to exchange the glory of the immortal God for images made to look like mortal man," especially when the image is the person in the mirror! We worship our own will as our highest authority. But by abandoning God, we become godless and soon after, we become wicked gods.

A WICKED ATTACK AGAINST VERA
AND THE GLORY OF GOD

Vera came to our pregnancy center as an eighteen-year-old unwed mother. She grew up in her grandfather's church in

Boston's inner city, where he is the pastor. Once I delivered a sermon entitled "How to Grow Up in the Church and Still Find God," because I know that even kids like Vera get confused and dragged away. Vera got involved with a young man who shared none of her faith and values. It didn't take long before Vera's values gave way. But the day she left our center, she made a small turnabout. She decided to keep her baby and start fresh with God, by His help.

Months later Vera came by with her three-month-old, beautiful baby son. We blessed her with many baby supplies and encouraged her to hold fast to God and her moral values. The notecard of her visit recorded by her counselor says she had adopted an abstinent lifestyle because of her recommitment to Christ and was attempting to break off the abusive relationship she had with the baby's father. She wanted a peaceful home.

She now has it, but it wasn't what we expected. A month after we blessed Vera with baby supplies, we had to help pay for her funeral. Vera was stabbed repeatedly with a knife and bled to death outside her apartment three blocks away from our center. After murdering Vera, her boyfriend attempted to rape another woman and was arrested. We wept and grieved with her family. Many wept aloud, "How could this happen?"

My answer, cutting below all the surface motives, would be that a man who was godless became a wicked god. When we do only what we want and what we feel, with no higher authority, we will eventually want to do wrong. Nobody will stop us, except by force.

His crime, however, is even greater than murder. He murdered Vera *and* defaced the glory of God she imaged. "You shall not murder," declares the sixth commandment. By this commandment God establishes the value He places on human life. The act of murder says, "God, what You call valuable, I call worthless. Your glory is worthless, and so is Your command." But what does God say? "I made Vera an image bearer of My own glory! I will not let you demean or deface My glory! I will utterly crush and defeat you and vindicate both Vera and My glory!" In other words, "The wrath of God is being revealed from heaven against all the godlessness and wickedness of men" (Romans 1:18).

GOD'S WRATH IS A SENSIBLE AND JUSTIFIED ANGER

God is justifiably angry when we treat Him with contempt by demeaning Him directly (by refusing to glorify Him as God) and defacing Him indirectly (by hurting people made in the image of His glory). We experience anger for similar reasons. For example, when someone defaces a Jewish gravestone with a painted swastika, society is right to be angry. We're not angry over the need to buy paint remover. We're angry because it defaces human life, and in this case, in a way that reasserts the evil of the Holocaust. Our wrath is necessary and healthy. Love must be able to get angry as well as to comfort.

For example, if I come across a man raping a woman, I cannot love both of them in the same way (and my point is that neither can God). Love is inherently *moral* in character and demands a moral force that is as much opposing as it is defending. I can't go up to the struggling, terrorized woman and the overpowering assailant and say, "I love you both just the same, and so does God. He doesn't want you to harm this girl, but please don't think He is angry at you right now. Because God is love, He doesn't get mad. Isn't such love amazing?" The woman would denounce my love as sick and worthless, even cowardly and evil. She would know that love must have a *passionate commitment* to right over wrong. It must be willing to vindicate and disarm; to reward and to punish. To act in love in this situation I must *hate* what the attacker is doing and push him aside, scream my lungs out for help, grab the woman, and run.

The punishment later dispensed in a court of law validates the respect and love we hold for the woman. It affirms her honor. It helps her heal from her wounds. Even in the course of our normal social life, we sense the rightness of holy anger. Consider how demeaned we can feel and offended we can become when someone merely slights us or ignores us. How quick we are to react, even though we aren't holy or all-glorious. Imagine, then, what an enormous offense it is to deface the glory of God by our evil behavior? The sin is as great as God's glory is great. This and nothing less than this is the degree of offense committed in every act of sin.[4] Therefore, David acknowledged to God,

> You are proved right when you speak
> and justified when you judge. (Psalm 51:4)

BACK TO THE DAY I STOLE A HAT

In the previous chapter, I told of the day I stole a hat. Let's go back a moment and apply what God says to my petty theft. The apostle Paul's response to me might go like this, "John, you have sinned against your fellow man, who is trying to provide for his family. You have hurt him and this is wrong. It's all the more wrong because God has commanded you to love your neighbor and you know this. By stealing you have said to God, 'Your commands mean nothing to me.' Your stealing also says to God, 'You can't be trusted to provide my happiness.' This is a great put-down of God, and it makes Him angry. Therefore, don't think that God's wrath is coming on you for stealing a three-dollar hat. It's coming on you for defying God's rightful authority over you. It's coming on you for demeaning God's *trustworthiness*. A just punishment for stealing a hat might be to return it and pay a fine of thirty dollars. But what is the just penalty for defacing the eternal glory of God except an eternal punishment?"

Our difficulty in seeing the enormity of this sin reflects how far our thoughts have sunk from the glory of God. Up until now we thought our problem was that God might not be impressed with us as much as we would like Him to be. We have a few bad marks on an otherwise good record. We've worried that even those few bad marks might cause us a problem with God—after all, He does have high standards. So we try to do a little "extra credit" work to impress Him. But in truth, the problem is that we have not been impressed with *Him*. We want God to marvel at us when, in reality, we ought to marvel at Him! That is the sin that damns us.

The implication is astounding! And Romans 14:23 confirms it. "Everything that does not come from faith is sin." To me, this is the most shocking truth in the Bible, because it completely demolishes any hope that God might be impressed with some of what I do and use that to form the basis of forgiving and accepting me. Instead, what is revealed is that *all* of what I do is forming the basis of my condemnation because all of what I do is done in an effort to supplant the glory of God with my own—and this is a form of robbery. Every second I put off living for the glory of God, I'm only adding to the justice of God's fierce wrath.

So the enormity of our sin consists of this exchange of affection from seeking the glory of God for a self-seeking glory. God declares, boldly and without apologies, that for those who are "self-seeking and who reject the truth and follow evil, there will be wrath and anger" (Romans 2:8).

THE WRATH OF GOD, WITHOUT APOLOGIES

Throughout Scripture God declares the fierceness of His wrath without apologies. Isaiah declared the certainty and intensity of it in 13:6-13.

> Wail, for the day of the LORD is near;
>   it will come like destruction from the Almighty.
> Because of this, all hands will go limp,
>   every man's heart will melt.
> Terror will seize them,
>   pain and anguish will grip them;
>   they will writhe like a woman in labor.
> They will look aghast at each other,
>   their faces aflame.
>
> See, the day of the Lord is coming
>   —a cruel day, with wrath and fierce anger—

to make the land desolate
and destroy the sinners within it.
The stars of heaven and their constellations
will not show their light.
The rising sun will be darkened
and the moon will not give its light.
I will punish the world for its evil,
the wicked for their sins. . . .
I will make man scarcer than pure gold,
more rare than the gold of Ophir.
Therefore I will make the heavens tremble;
and the earth will shake from its place
at the wrath of the LORD Almighty,
in the day of His burning anger.

Zephaniah described the bitterness of God's wrath in 1:14-15,17.

"The great day of the LORD is near—
near and coming quickly.
Listen! The cry on the day of the LORD will be bitter,
the shouting of the warrior there.
That day will be a day of wrath,
a day of distress and anguish,
a day of trouble and ruin, . . .
because they have sinned against the LORD."

Lest we delude ourselves that wrath is a feature of only the Old Testament God and that, in the New Testament, God has improved on His character somehow, we can read:

Of this you can be sure: No immoral, impure or greedy person—such a [person] is an idolater—has any inheritance in the kingdom of Christ and of God. Let no one deceive you with empty words, for because of such things God's wrath comes on those who are disobedient. (Ephesians 5:5-6)

God's wrath is described as "fierce" (1 Samuel 28:18), furious (Job 40:11), "full" (Psalm 78:38), "consuming" (Psalm 59:13), "great" (Psalm 102:10), and "jealous" (Ezekiel 36:6). Various images are used to describe God's wrath, all of which succeed in impressing on our unbelieving and disobedient hearts that it's a mistake with severe consequences to make God our enemy. In Isaiah 10:5, God warns the sinful nation of Assyria that His wrath is akin to being struck down in a battle:

"Woe to the Assyrian, the rod of my anger,
    in whose hand is the club of my wrath!"

God's wrath is compared to a winepress in Revelation 14:19-20. "The angel swung his sickle on the earth, gathered its grapes and threw them into the great winepress of God's wrath. They were trampled in the winepress outside the city, and blood flowed out of the press."

The most commonly used metaphor for God's wrath is fire—consuming and painful. Touch your hand to a hot stove and the response is swift. Consider then the wrath of God.

In His wrath the LORD will swallow them up,
    and His fire will consume them. (Psalm 21:9)

He has poured out His wrath like fire
    on the tent of the Daughter of Zion.
    (Lamentations 2:4)

Who can withstand His indignation?
    Who can endure His fierce anger?
His wrath is poured out like fire;
    the rocks are shattered before Him.
    (Nahum 1:6)

There comes a day when God deals with our sins. When it comes, it feels like fire.

THE WRATH OF GOD ACCORDING TO JESUS CHRIST

The most terrifying words of divine wrath revealed in the Bible, however, come from the mouth of Jesus—and properly so. As W. G. T. Shedd wrote,

> As none but God has the right and would dare to sentence a soul to eternal misery for sin . . . so none but God has the right and should presume to delineate the nature and consequences of this sentence. This is the reason why most of the awful imagery in which the sufferings of the wicked are described is found in the discourses of our Lord and Savior.[5]

Speaking of that day when all people are summoned before Him for judgment, Jesus said He will say to the self-seeking, "Depart from me, you who are cursed, into the eternal fire prepared for the devil and his angels. For I was hungry and you gave me nothing to eat, I was thirsty and you gave me nothing to drink" (Matthew 25:41-42). He warned us to take repentance seriously by warning of the awful torments of hell.

> If your eye causes you to sin, pluck it out. It is better for you to enter the kingdom of God with one eye than to have two eyes and be thrown into hell, where
>
> "their worm does not die,
> and the fire is not quenched." (Mark 9:47-48)

To Jesus Christ, hell is God's wrath with no admixture of mercy. Hell represents God's *final* condemnation when unbelief and defiance have reached full maturity. Hell signals that there is a time when God's patience with unrepentant sinners runs out. Notice I said *unrepentant* sinners. Hell assures us that there comes a time when God conquers the wicked because they will not turn and seek His forgiveness.

Hell is, according to Jesus, the worst condemnation imaginable. Its purpose is not remedial but punitive. The punishment is not temporary but eternal. Jesus said, "Then they will go away

71

to *eternal punishment*, but the righteous to eternal life" (Matthew 25:46).[6] It's not a question of losing your soul, but *body* and soul. Jesus warned us, "Do not be afraid of those who kill the body but cannot kill the soul. Rather, be afraid of the One who can destroy both soul and body in hell" (Matthew 10:28).

While hell itself is not corrective, the warnings of hell are so intended. Jesus reveals the horrors of the fire of hell to convince us to take our sin seriously and to show us clearly that we need to turn from our sin and seek the forgiveness of God. Where these fail, nothing is left over but punishment.

TWO COMMON MISCONCEPTIONS ABOUT THE JUDGMENT OF GOD

Several years ago I attended an evangelistic crusade. The preacher clearly wanted to bring people into a personal relationship with Jesus Christ. He wanted to affirm the loving-kindness of Christ, and at the same time affirm the reality of hell. The two appeared incompatible. So the preacher explained, "God does not send people to hell. They choose to go there." This view has the immediate benefit of affirming that hell is real without staining God's love and desire to save people. But I think the statement is distorted. It contains two common misconceptions.

First, the Bible does not generally use the term *people* with reference to God's judgment. The term *people* is used to describe our commonness as created beings without any reference to our moral character. We talk of the people in our neighborhood. Our coworkers are people. People make up a crowd gathered in a football stadium, or an entire city or nation—the Chinese people, for example. No moral distinctions are made. Nothing is known or stated about any individual's moral goodness.[7] It's people we see dying of starvation. We're moved because we see them as fellow human beings made in the image of God.

When speaking of God's final judgment, the Bible uses a variety of terms that reflects the substance and foundation of our moral nature. We are called the "righteous" or the "wicked." God's judgment is not on people but on the *wicked*. So we read in Proverbs 2:22 that the "wicked will be cut off from the land," and in 3:33 that

The LORD's curse is on the house of the wicked,
    but He blesses the home of the righteous.

Jesus said, "At the end of the age . . . angels will come and separate the wicked from the righteous and throw them into the fiery furnace, where there will be weeping and gnashing of teeth" (Matthew 13:49-50). God will separate the "wheat" from the "weeds," and the "good fish" from the "bad [fish]," and the "sheep" from the "goats" (Matthew 13:36-42,47-48, 25:32). It's the "wicked [that] will not inherit the kingdom of God" (1 Corinthians 6:9). Instead,

On the wicked He will rain
    fiery coals and burning sulfur;
    a scorching wind will be their lot.

For the LORD is righteous,
    He loves justice;
    upright men will see His face. (Psalm 11:6-7)

So, when we hear about a planeload of people dying in a crash, without knowing any of them personally, we grieve. We think of their pain, the sorrow of their families, etc. Suppose, however, that we know what young twelve-year-old Susan knows: that her father, the man in seat 23C, has been molesting her for two years and plans to do so that evening when he gets home. If we did know this, we might weep in relief that a *wicked* man is no longer alive to destroy a young innocent life. Our ability to sympathize or grieve over someone's death is largely guided by this judicial sentiment.

When we speak of God's wrath coming on *people* rather than on the *wicked*, we inevitably sense a oneness with them rather than with God. But this puts us in opposition to God and the righteousness of His ways. Therefore, this difference in the language we use is important. The *righteous* long to be free of the Devil and all his harassments. The righteous long to see God bring down His impenitent enemies. They long to live in a place where there is no rape and theft and murder, nor their subtle counterparts: manipulation, exploitation, and slander.

The Lord even *comforts* the righteous, who suffer at the hands of wicked men, with the knowledge of His coming wrath. Second Thessalonians 1:5-10 says,

> All this is evidence that God's judgment is right, and as a result you will be counted worthy of the kingdom of God, for which you are suffering. God is just: He will pay back trouble to those who trouble you and give relief to you who are troubled, and to us as well. This will happen when the Lord Jesus is revealed from heaven in blazing fire with His powerful angels. He will punish those who do not know God and do not obey the gospel of our Lord Jesus. They will be punished with everlasting destruction and shut out from the presence of the Lord and from the majesty of His power on the day He comes to be glorified in His holy people and to be marveled at among all those who have believed.

The other misconception deals with whether the wicked choose hell or not. It's more accurate to say they choose to reject heaven. If we reject God and His supremacy, if we live to deface His glory, then heaven is the last place we would enjoy. But the wicked *never* choose hell. They go there against their will, "weeping and gnashing [their] teeth" (Matthew 25:30). In all of God's judgment, God, boldly and without apology, takes an active role, not a passive one. The wicked do not leap or fall into the lake of fire. They are *thrown* into it, on purpose, according to the perfect righteousness of God. "If anyone's name was not found written in the book of life, he was thrown into the lake of fire" (Revelation 20:15).

ACKNOWLEDGING OUR TRUE NEED FOR FORGIVENESS

None of what Jesus said or did will make any sense later on unless God painfully and deeply cuts into our natural pride *first* and makes us sensible of our genuine need for forgiveness. Jesus drove the point home when He said to the Pharisees, "How will you escape being condemned to hell?" (Matthew 23:33). If Jesus can say this to the Pharisees, who lived a strict moral life by human standards, then it should lead us to despair of any hope that our own goodness will impress God and form the basis of His forgiveness. It won't. We need God's forgiveness.

When Job questioned the fairness of God's judgment instead of acknowledging his need for forgiveness, the Lord responded,

> "Who is this that darkens my counsel
> with words without knowledge?" (Job 38:2)

Then He added, in 40:7-14:

> "Brace yourself like a man;
> I will question you,
> and you shall answer me.
>
> Would you discredit my justice?
> Would you condemn me to justify yourself?
> Do you have an arm like God's,
> and can your voice thunder like His?
> Then adorn yourself with glory and splendor,
> and clothe yourself in honor and majesty.
> Unleash the fury of your wrath,
> look at every proud man and bring him low,
> look at every proud man and humble him,
> crush the wicked where they stand.
> Bury them all in the dust together;
> shroud their faces in the grave.
> Then I myself will admit to you
> that your own right hand can save you."

It's dimwitted for Job to accuse God of injustice as a ploy to justify himself. But we're all guilty of this; it's one of our first lines of defense. We're stupid enough to think that God will go all gushy on us. God doesn't sweat the threat that says, "You're not really a good God if you follow through on any of this wrath business!" He doesn't say, "Oh, I'm sorry. I'm really a good guy, really I am. I guess you're right and I was wrong. It would be unloving if I were to get angry and punish you for your wickedness. Thank you for your probing insight. You can rest assured that all this business about wrath will not be brought up again."

God's response to Job has a tinge of divine sarcasm in it. God is quite confident that His wrath is in keeping with both His justice and His love, even if we don't see it. Even more, He is unapologetic about the fierceness of His wrath. He is sworn to "unleash the fury of [His] wrath" and to "crush" the wicked and to "bury" them in the dust. No apology is given. No defense is offered. God even glories in the power of His wrath and the victory He will have in crushing the wicked. He's boasting in His own majesty as the glorious God that He is, and in effect, challenging Job, saying, "Are *you* a glorious and majestic God? Then show Me your *wrath!*" God sees His fierce wrath as part of His glory! He points the finger back at Job and says in effect, "If you think you make a better God than Me, then stay the course you're on. Save yourself, then I'll be impressed with you." Only a fool would try. Job relented. We would do well to follow Job. What we need to do is acknowledge the justice of God's judgment and admit our true need for His forgiveness.

King David did. He acknowledged that all the sins he committed boiled down to one wretched and damnable sin: defying God's rule over his life. He demeaned and defaced the glory of God. In Psalm 51:4 he prayed and confessed,

> Against you, you only, have I sinned
> and done what is evil in your sight,
> so that you are proved right when you speak
> and justified when you judge.

In so praying we are agreeing with God and our conscience that what we have done deserves the wrath of God. We are renouncing self-centered living and turning to God-centered living. This moves us forward from guilt to gladness.

❧

The Journey from Guilt to Gladness

The biblical revelation of God's severity suggests that our guilt is deeper than we ever knew and that our need for forgiveness is greater than we ever knew. Owning up to this by acknowledging the justice of God's judgment is the next step from guilt to gladness.

Chapter Four

Forgiveness Promised

PUTTING OUR HOPE IN GOD

I feel my shame inside me like a knife.
He told me I had a soul.
How does he know?
What spirit comes to move my life?
Is there another way to go?
—VALJEAN, IN *LES MISÉRABLES*

☙

The LORD delights in those who fear Him,
who put their hope in His unfailing love.
—PSALM 147:11

Charles Simeon (1758-1836) once wrote, "The truth is not in the middle and not in one extreme, but in both extremes."[1] Perhaps he was reading Romans 11:22: "Behold then the kindness and severity of God" (NASB). God's response to our guilt is not somewhere between wrath and kindness, and it's not one or the other. His response is extreme wrath *and* extreme kindness.

In the last chapter we looked at the severity of God's wrath. Now we turn to the depth of God's kindness and ask: What hope is there for me? Can God forgive me? How can He do so? Under what conditions does He forgive? What we will see is that without injuring God's justice, God's loving-kindness is at work to bring forgiveness and freedom to all who put their hope in His unfailing love. Therefore the next step from guilt to gladness is to put our hope in God.

ANOREXIA OF THE SOUL

This hope is not wishful thinking, nor mere optimism. In truth it's born out of a deep and genuine conviction of the awfulness of our actions. The biblical phrase for this is "godly sorrow." Its counterpart is despair. The two share a certain degree of pain and anguish over the evilness of our sinful behavior. The difference, however, is that one leads to repentance and renewal while the other leads to hopelessness and death. Notice how they are described in 2 Corinthians 7:10: "Godly sorrow produces repentance [that leads] to salvation, not to be regretted; but the sorrow of the world produces death" (NKJV).

What is this worldly sorrow? We get a clue from 1 Thessalonians 4:13. The apostle Paul writes, "But I do not want you to be ignorant, brethren, concerning those who have fallen asleep, lest you sorrow as others who have no hope" (NKJV). "Worldly sorrow" is *sorrow with no hope in it*—which also is an accurate definition of despair. Once we're finally convinced that we need God's forgiveness, we can become firmly convinced that we can never obtain it. We leap from denial right into despair. But ongoing, immovable despair under the conviction of sin and guilt leads to death. I call it anorexia of the soul.

An anorectic is firmly convinced (deceived really) that eating food, the very source of life, is bad for her and will make her worse than she already is. Even as she starves herself, shrinking to skin and bones, she loathes eating. Without intervention, this sickness leads to death.

Despair works like anorexia—but in the soul. We slowly starve ourselves to death because the very source of nourishment, the God of infinite glory and abundant life, has become in our mind's eye, poison. Søren Kierkegaard even titled his book on despair *The Sickness unto Death*, concluding that "the despairing man is mortally ill."[2] He's echoing Paul's warning that worldly sorrow produces death.

In contrast to despair, there is a God-inflicted, painful sorrow over sin that is not deadly because the tears are leavened with hope in God. Our conviction of sin causes us to sorrow before God, not run from God. Our shame causes us to turn to God in repentant faith, rather than run from God into further dissipation and ruin. It weeps, but because it also hopes, these tears eventually yield to the joy of our salvation. It leads "to salvation" and is "not to be regretted."

FRANK AT THE CROSSROADS OF HOPE AND DESPAIR

Frank describes himself as a "lapsed" Catholic. "The more I lived in the world," he told me, "the more irrelevant and unreal Christianity became. After I studied literary criticism in college, I lost hope that the Bible could be relied upon as a guide to know God. Now I'm not sure what to believe or who to believe."

Frank was at a point in his life where he wanted to find the truth and relevance of his childhood faith. I suggested he take a childlike approach. "Ask God to teach you and read His Word with a teachable heart." After that we stayed in touch through electronic mail. One day I sent him Psalm 147:11 with this hastily written note:

> The LORD delights in those who fear Him,
>> who put their hope in His unfailing love.

> Frank, the Lord doesn't hold a grudge. He could play "hard to get" when we finally call out to Him. Instead, when He sees us turn with a searching heart, no matter how confused we are or what our starting point is, He experiences great delight in this one thing, we have *turned to Him* for some instruction, with a sense of dependence on Him (hope). Clearly He delights in our hope in Him.

Frank E-mailed me back the next day.

> Thank you for the encouragement. I have tried to put the thoughts I have had in the past (such as: "it's too late," "too much has happened," "why should He?" etc.) out of my head, and approach God honestly: as one who knows his past wasn't always correct, who wants to correct it.[3]

Frank confirmed how common it is for people to get bogged down in despair once they sense the sinfulness of

unbelief. In *Pilgrim's Progress*, John Bunyan's allegorical out-
line of Christian experience, the first obstacle the young Pilgrim encounters as he starts his journey toward the Celestial
City is the "slough of despond." Frank's letter showed me that
he had arrived at this sticky point. A spark of desire within
and a growing conviction regarding his unfaithfulness compelled him to look toward God. But the same burden tempted
him to ask, "Is there any realistic hope for me?" Like Frank,
we all tend to leap from denial to despair because we can see
no way for God to forgive without making a mockery of His
holiness and justice. But since both denial and despair lead
to death, the only way to pass through this painful season of
regret and sorrow is to put our hope in God.

BIBLICAL HOPE IS NOT FOR UNIVERSAL FORGIVENESS

In putting our hope in God, we are not hoping that God will
forgive us simply because He must. Biblical hope is fully cog-
nizant that God does not forgive everyone. It doesn't say, "Ah,
God is loving. He must forgive everyone." No such hope is found
in Scripture. Biblical hope trusts in the true and sovereign God,
who has declared, "I will have mercy on whom I will have mercy,
and I will have compassion on whom I will have compassion"
(Exodus 33:19). This is God's claim to fame; He alone is sovereign. He has an absolutely free will. This, God declares (again
without apology), is what makes Him God!

> Our God is in heaven;
> He does whatever pleases Him. (Psalm 115:3)

His sovereignty includes the right to give His mercy to some
without being obligated to give it to all.

For example, God did forgive Noah but not the people of
Noah's day:

> The LORD saw how great man's wickedness on the earth
> had become, and that every inclination of the thoughts of

his heart was only evil all the time. . . . The LORD said, "I will wipe mankind, whom I have created from the face of the earth—men and animals, and creatures that move along the ground, and birds of the air—for I am grieved that I have made them." But Noah found favor in the eyes of the LORD. (Genesis 6:5-8)

Noah's generation grew so wicked that God wiped it out. Noah and his family received grace; the others got what their wickedness deserved.

God did not forgive the morally bankrupt people of Sodom and Gomorrah. Their sense of moral decency had sunk so low that it was permissible for a group of men to attempt to gang-rape two male visitors to their town. What they didn't know was that the two men were servants of God (angels) sent to Lot to warn him to flee the coming judgment. God had endured enough. The horrific treatment the servants received signified how mature the people's rebellion and wickedness had grown. The two servants of God said to Lot,

The outcry to the LORD against its people is so great that He has sent us to destroy it. . . . Hurry! Take your wife and your two daughters who are here, or you will be swept away when the city is punished. (Genesis 19:13,15)

Lot experienced God's kindness (16,19). As for the rest, "The LORD rained down burning sulfur on Sodom and Gomorrah—from the LORD out of the heavens" (24).

Pharaoh is another example of someone God did not forgive. "Let My people go!" God commanded. Pharaoh clenched his fist and defied God. "Who is the LORD, that I should obey Him . . . ? I do not know the LORD and I will not let Israel go" (Exodus 5:2). God separated the sea for the people of Israel to escape the rushing army of Pharaoh. When Pharaoh and his men pursued them, the sea swept in and destroyed them all. In Exodus 14:18 God said, "The Egyptians will know that I am the LORD when I gain glory through Pharaoh, his chariots and his horsemen." God gained glory in their destruction.

Joshua led Israel into the Promised Land with a severe warning. "He is a holy God; He is a jealous God. *He will not forgive your rebellion and your sins.* If you forsake the LORD and serve foreign gods, He will turn and bring disaster on you and make an end of you, after He has been good to you" (Joshua 24:19-20,). This was a negative promise from God, a warning not to presume God has to forgive.

Joshua's warning came to pass in the days of Manasseh, king of Judah, when the people's rebellion and sin reached their zenith in sacrificing precious children to false gods (2 Chronicles 33:6). God took away the Promised Land from the people He promised it to, because they broke the conditions of the promise (abiding faith). He handed the land over to the king of Babylon, who killed many and exiled the rest. Lest there be any doubt that this was God's doing, this passage was recorded:

> Surely these things happened to Judah according to the LORD's command, in order to remove them from His presence because of the sins of Manasseh and all he had done, including the shedding of innocent blood. For he had filled Jerusalem with innocent blood, *and the LORD was not willing to forgive.* (2 Kings 24:3-4)

The leaders of Israel who failed to defend the weak and rescue the poor were not forgiven (Jeremiah 5:27-29). Jesus warned the Pharisees that God would not forgive them for their self-righteousness and hypocrisy (Luke 11:42-52). Judas was not forgiven (Acts 1:25). Our hope in God clearly recognizes that God does not forgive everyone. He is under no obligation to forgive the wicked. Therefore, it's appropriate that we should wrestle under the conviction of our guilt with the question, What hope is there for me? It's a life-changing question if we hang with it long enough to find the answer. John Newton did, and he ended up changing the whole world when he discovered the answer.

WHAT HAPPENED WHEN JOHN NEWTON
PUT HIS HOPE IN GOD

On March 9, 1748, John Newton (1725–1807) was in the midst of a violent storm at sea. Gigantic waves pounded and thrashed his ship, *The Greyhound.* One side of the ship was so battered and the water was rushing in so fast that men despaired of their lives. All hands were preparing to die, including Newton. He was only twenty-three years old.

Newton was raised by a godly mother who died when he was seven. His exposure to the vital Christian faith ended there. At eleven John's father took him to sea. By the time he was twenty-three and sailing into the storm, he had a wide, well-founded reputation for being lazy, lustful, rebellious, and crude. He despised the "weakness" of Christians and loved to destroy the faith of any sailors who came on board. He prided himself in being the instigator of everything obscene. In his own words, "my life was one of continual godlessness and profanity. I do not know that I ever met a man with a mouth more vile than my own." Looking back on his youth, Newton later wrote, "Not only did I sin, but I got others to sin with me."[4]

The ship captain was especially offended by Newton's crude and blasphemous jokes against the Christian faith. When the storm hit, the captain cursed Newton as a "Jonah." The other sailors would have gladly thrown him overboard except that Newton was manning the pumps on that ferocious night at sea. The captain knew that if he could not turn the ship around to ease the stress on the battered side, they would sink with the next gigantic wave. According to Peter Masters' biographical sketch of Newton,

> [John Newton] turned to look at the flooded area of the ship which he had been pumping. "If that won't do," he said, "the Lord have mercy on us." Suddenly, for the first time in years, his blasphemous words seemed to bite back at him. "What mercy do I deserve?" he thought. The answer seemed painfully obvious.

The color drained from his face and his mocking, arrogant manner gave way to deep fear and clamoring thoughts. . . . How could he face the God whom he had insulted for so long? He began to feel a crushing despair.[5]

The ship did not sink. The sobering questions raised in John's mind gripped him even when the calm returned. In the privacy of his quarters he started to read the Scriptures to understand what hope he might have for obtaining God's forgiveness. Godly sorrow was producing true repentance.

To zoom forward, John Newton lived eighty-two years and became an oak tree of righteousness. He developed a passion for the worship of God, as the hymn he wrote, "Amazing Grace," testifies. He became a man of the Book and a herald of the good news of the gospel. He was ordained into the Anglican Church, preaching and testifying for decades. He became a man of compassion — personally supporting and caring for the poet William Cowper through his many years of mental illness and suicide attempts. Newton became a man of moral courage in confronting public injustice as well.

In his seafaring days, Newton sailed on slave ships, even becoming the captain of one, where he saw firsthand the inhumanity of that wretched traffic. Years later he wrote a book denouncing the slave trade to help William Wilberforce, a member of Parliament, in his crusade to abolish it in England.

Newton is a testimony to what the grace of God can accomplish in a person's life. But grace begins as a heartfelt experience when we ask, "Can God forgive me?" Newton's question could have led to hopeless despair and eternal death. Instead he turned to God in godly sorrow over his sin. This led to a repentance that transformed his whole life and changed the world forever.

GOD HAS A HEART TO FORGIVE

God has made it abundantly clear that while He does not forgive everyone, He has a heart to forgive. If we could see God, we would see that He is by nature a God of loving-kindness who is able to forgive great wickedness. We know this because Moses once asked to see God (Exodus 33:18). And God said, "Fine." Exodus 34:6-7 says,

> [God] passed in front of Moses, proclaiming, "The LORD, the LORD, the compassionate and gracious God, slow to anger, abounding in love and faithfulness, maintaining love to thousands, and forgiving wickedness, rebellion and sin. Yet He does not leave the guilty unpunished."

We have yet to answer *how* God punishes the guilty and yet forgives the wickedness of thousands, but we're coming to that. First we must see that He has a heart to do it. The Lord *is* gracious. The Lord *is* abounding in love. He *is* willing to forgive the wickedness, rebellion, and sin of thousands! Behold the wonder of God's kindness!

Psalm 63:3 says of God,

> Because Your lovingkindness is better than life,
> My lips shall praise You. (NKJV)

The foundation of our hope for obtaining God's forgiveness is God's loving-kindness. If this isn't God's heart, despair is justified. Because it is, beholding God's loving-kindness is our weapon in the battle against despair.

GOD'S JUDGMENT COMES ONLY AS A LAST RESORT

In cities like Boston, young rebels pride themselves on their short tempers. A wrong look is taken as a grave personal insult and injury. Gunfire is returned for an insult. They're like Lamech, who wrote the first "gangsta" rap song.

> I have killed a man for wounding me,
>   a young man for injuring me.

If Cain is avenged seven times,
then Lamech seventy-seven times. (Genesis 4:23-24)

In contrast, God is slow to anger; His punishment comes as a *last* resort after many warnings. In Noah's day God saw that "every inclination of the thoughts of [man's] heart was only evil all the time" (Genesis 6:5). God's judgment did not come when the people first sinned or even when their wickedness grew to full maturity. He endured 120 more years of their all-pervasive wickedness, warning them throughout to repent, before He finally said, "Enough" (6:3). Even as Noah banged away on the ark, he warned them to turn their hearts to God. When they did not repent, the floodgates were released.

God did not forgive Pharaoh, but remember, for *four hundred years* the Israelites prayed for deliverance from the oppression of the Egyptians. God heard their cries and was concerned about their suffering (Exodus 3:7). They had to suffer long because God is long-suffering with the wicked. Even when He finally came to judge Egypt and deliver Israel, He approached Pharaoh over *ten times* before His wrath was finally unleashed.

Judas' hypocrisy was patiently endured by Jesus for three years, and not just any three years. Judas saw Jesus healing the blind and raising the dead. He heard the kingdom of God proclaimed. What about God's judgment on the Pharisees and the other leaders of Jerusalem? Jesus wept over Jerusalem (Luke 19:41). Their hardness of heart meant they would not know the forgiveness of God, though He was inclined to give it.

God prefers mercy over judgment: "As surely as I live, declares the Sovereign LORD, I take no pleasure in the death of the wicked, but rather that they turn from their ways and live. Turn! Turn from your evil ways! Why will you die, O house of Israel?" (Ezekiel 33:11). This is the heart of God.

Though He brings grief, He will show compassion,
so great is His unfailing love.

He does not *willingly* bring affliction
   or grief to the children of men. (Lamentations
3:32-33)

Daniel Fuller calls judgment the penultimate (next-to-last) desire of God's heart.

We may sum up the relationship between God's love and wrath with the statement, so vital for understanding His plan in redemptive history, that God's kindness . . . is His free, ultimate work in which His soul finally and fully delights, whereas God's wrath in punishment is His neces-sary, penultimate work. Though He finds no pleasure in punishing the wicked, He nevertheless does it as some-thing He must do, so that without devaluing His glory, He can fully rejoice in being merciful to the penitent.[6]

I recently served on a jury trial. The man on trial had been caught selling crack cocaine. He had a "domestic partner" and a couple of children. But he was a drug dealer, and many moth-ers in the tenement lamented for the well-being of their chil-dren. When I looked at the man's "wife" I felt sad for her. I thought of his small children and wondered what was going to happen to this poor family now. It troubled me to do my duty and render a just and correct verdict, because he was truly guilty according to the evidence. I grieved that I had to convict him and send him to jail. In this sense, God also grieves. He doesn't delight in punishment per se.

But there was more to look at than just the man and his family. I looked at the housing project he lived in, and the many poor families desperately crying out for city leaders to remove drugs and dealers from their area. Poor mothers love their children and desire their protection just as much as other classes do. I thought of the pain they would bear if I let him go. I could anticipate their joy should he be removed. So I could feel pain and pleasure at the same time, depending on my focus.

God's emotions have a similarly bifocal quality. In Ezekiel 18:32 He says, "I take no pleasure in the death of anyone." Deuteronomy 28:63 states that "it will please [God] to ruin and destroy you." Clearly God can grieve for one reason (love for His creation) over something that He does (judgment) that for another reason (love for His name and His people) He delights to do.

WHOM DOES GOD FORGIVE?

Whom does God forgive and under what conditions does He forgive? God forgives those who put their hope in the very God who condemns them for their wickedness.

> The LORD delights in those who fear Him,
>   who put their hope in His unfailing love.
> (Psalm 147:11)

> The LORD is good to those whose hope is in Him.
> (Lamentations 3:25)

If you ask me *how* to put your hope in God, I would refer you to the variety of descriptions in Scripture that calls for a shift in the heart's affections from sin and self to God and His work on your behalf. To hope in God is to *trust* in the Lord (Psalm 32:10); *humble* yourselves before the Lord (Proverbs 3:34); *wait* for the Lord (Isaiah 30:18); *fear* the Lord (Psalm 31:19); *love* the Lord (Exodus 20:5-6); *turn* to the Lord (Isaiah 55:7); *take refuge* in the Lord (Psalm 31:19); *seek* the Lord (Psalm 34:10); *repent* (Isaiah 59:20); and *have faith* in the Lord (2 Chronicles 20:20). Those who do are the objects of God's loving-kindness.

In Psalm 33:18-22 the answers come in rapid-fire repetition.

> But the eyes of the LORD are on those who *fear* Him,
>   on those whose *hope* is in His unfailing love,
> to deliver them from death. . . .

We *wait* in hope for the LORD;
    He is our help and our shield.
In Him our hearts rejoice,
    for we *trust* in His holy name.
May your unfailing love rest upon us, O LORD,
    even as *we put our hope in you.*

In 2 Chronicles 30:9 the answer is, "The LORD your God is *gracious and merciful,* and will not turn His face from you *if you return to Him*" (NKJV). In Psalm 86:5 the answer is,

You are forgiving and good, O Lord,
    abounding in *love* to all who *call to you.*

Clearly it's not simply *sinning that damns us.* It's sinning and not repenting. Despair is appropriate *only* for unrepentant, obstinate sinners who refuse to turn their hearts toward God. Romans 2:5-8 says, "Because of your *stubbornness* and your *unrepentant heart,* you are storing up wrath against yourself for the day of God's wrath, when His righteous judgments will be revealed." Contrast this with Joel 2:12-13:

"Even now," declares the LORD,
    "return to me with all your heart,
    with fasting and weeping and mourning."

Rend your heart
    and not your garments.
Return to the LORD your God,
    for He is gracious and compassionate,
slow to anger and abounding in love,
    and He relents from sending calamity.

This is a clarion call to put our hope in God. To personalize it, this means that I look to God's loving-kindness and trust that while He is right to be angry and just to condemn me, His kindness is so extraordinary that He Himself will make a way for His forgiveness to flow to me and restore our broken relationship. I may not yet understand how God can show me mercy without compromising His justice, but I trust that He does know.

> The LORD *loves righteousness and justice;*
>   the earth is full of His *unfailing love.* (Psalm 33:5)

He will uphold both justice and kindness in my salvation.

GOD HAS A MIRACLE PLANNED

When we put our hope in God, we are really waiting and watching for God *to provide a miracle on our behalf.* To hope means to trust that God has a plan to execute His punishment against us and extend His pardon to us at the same time. This very plan was first revealed to Abraham. God told Abraham, "Take your son, your only son, Isaac, whom you love, and go to the region of Moriah. Sacrifice him there as a burnt offering" (Genesis 22:2). Abraham obeyed. Why did God command Abraham to do this? First, to test the substance of his faith, whether it was full of trust and dependence and obedience, or whether it was a worthless and false faith (22:1,12). But second, to teach Abraham and all who came after him that God had a plan to provide a substitute punishment for sin. When Abraham had the knife ready, God called him to stop, commended him for his obedient faith, and then pointed out the lesson.

> Abraham looked up and there in a thicket he saw a ram caught by its horns. He went over and took the ram and sacrificed it as a burnt offering instead of his son. So Abraham called that place The LORD Will Provide. And to this day it is said, "On the mountain of the LORD it will be provided." (22:13-14)

Abraham learned and trusted—"On the mountain of the LORD it will be provided." Mount Moriah is not mentioned again until the days of Israel's greatest king, Solomon. Then, lo and behold, "Solomon began to build the temple of the LORD in Jerusalem on Mount Moriah" (2 Chronicles 3:1). Where? On Mount Moriah in Jerusalem. Abraham's mountain! Centuries after Abraham first learned that God would provide a substitute on this mountain the temple was built there, and for centuries to come millions of animal sacrifices would be made on Mount Moriah, daily reminding the people that a substitute punishment for sin was needed and would be provided one day by God.

When that day came God led His Son, His only Son, His beloved Son to the very same spot. Matthew 16:21 says, "Jesus began to explain to His disciples that He must go to Jerusalem and suffer many things at the hands of the elders, chief priests and teachers of the law, and that He must be killed and on the third day be raised to life." Why Jerusalem? Because God promised those who hope in Him that *on the mountain of the Lord it would be provided.* I doubt that Abraham ever fully understood why he was commanded to take his son up the mountain as an offering. That is for us to savor as we turn now to the gospel of Jesus Christ—the gift of God.

∞

The Journey from Guilt to Gladness

We move from guilt toward gladness when we put our hope in God by looking to His loving-kindness and trusting that He has a way planned to forgive our sins and restore our broken relationship with Him, without injuring His righteousness.

Part Two
God's Gift

Chapter Five

Forgiveness Revealed

DISCOVERING CHRIST AS RESCUER

It is unworthy of God to unite himself to wretched man,
yet it is not unworthy of God to lift man up out of his wretchedness.
—BLAISE PASCAL, *PENSEÉS*

✿

[God] has rescued us from the dominion of darkness
and brought us into the kingdom of the Son He loves,
in whom we have redemption, the forgiveness of sins.
—COLOSSIANS 1:13-14

Magalie was illegally brought from Haiti to Boston by her father, through Canada, when she was thirteen years old. She graduated from high school five years later. Then her father abandoned her to take up with his new wife. When my staff and I met Magalie, she had no place to live or means of support. Because she was an illegal alien, she could not get a job—and she was pregnant by a man who did not want to provide for her and their child. Abandoned and desperate, she thought of getting rid of her baby. Instead, she drank ammonia to end her own life. We were able to intervene and help her. Seven months later, she gave birth to a beautiful son.

I couldn't get her a job though, because obtaining a green card, the legal permit to work, is a long and expensive process. A "friend" offered to help Magalie obtain working papers for five hundred dollars. She borrowed the money and signed the papers he prepared for her. At the court hearing, the judge asked Magalie a series of questions based on those documents. She immediately realized that the man who took her money had falsified the entire story of her life to get her "political asylum." She didn't want to lie to the judge, and since she could not validate her claim for political asylum, he immediately set a deportation hearing date.

In tears, Magalie called me and asked if I would go with her to her deportation hearing, since she could not afford a lawyer. I had her sit down and write the true story of her life. I had her "agree with her accuser" that she had misled the court by signing false statements. I had her ask the court to help her understand what the right and proper steps were for obtaining working papers in this country, with the pledge that she would work hard to provide for herself and her son if given a chance. To this I added my own letter.

Into the courtroom we walked. The seal of the United States government was in the center of the bench commanding respect and emanating authority. The judge sat above us in his formal black robe. Microphones and recorders noted every word spoken "for the record." Magalie trembled in her seat below the judge. He spoke deliberately, from rote, demonstrating that he had been through this process many times. With each answer Magalie drew one step closer to expulsion. In broken English, she finally told the judge that the document before him was false and that she had written her true story and would like to submit it to him. The judge stopped the proceedings and went "off the record" to read over her story and my accompanying letter.

I saw before me a judge who was used to being lied to, and who was committed to honor the laws of the land. I witnessed him set deportation dates for the two cases heard before Magalie's. He impressed me as a man governed by a sense of integrity and justice. Although principled, he was definitely not cold-hearted, for he was willing to let Magalie say what she had to say, no matter how broken her English was. He read her story and my letter. A copy was given to the government's lawyer at the next table, whose job it was to deport illegals. I held my breath and prayed. How could justice and mercy *both* be upheld?

The judge turned to Magalie and instructed her as to the forms she would have to fill out and return in order to apply for a work permit. *Grace!* I thought to myself. He advised her—no, he *urged* her—to get a lawyer to oversee the process. Magalie confessed that she had no money for a lawyer and that several *pro bono* places had turned down her case already (probably because of the fraudulent documents). Magalie could not save herself, even with the court's instructions and patience. The judge shook his head in frustration. He was clearly considering what more, if anything, he was willing to do.

Suddenly he turned to the clerk and instructed her to go immediately to his office and retrieve the phone number of his *personal* friend. Then he turned to Magalie. "Call him and tell him *I* told you to call," said the judge. "He will provide you a lawyer for free." Then he told her plainly that if she failed to call and follow his guidance and return the forms he needed, he would summarily deport her within thirty days after the date set for the next hearing.

The judge wanted to show kindness to Magalie. But to ensure that it would not compromise the law (and therefore his integrity as one sworn to uphold it), he sent his own personal friend to help bring Magalie into conformity with the law so that his stay of deportation would be legal and justified. *He was working to win her the right to live here lawfully.* For the first time, I could envision Magalie going to work every day and making a quiet life for herself and her son without fear. The judge was as aware as I of how gracious his help was. If she rejected it, he would rightly have applied the law without mercy, and deported her.

I sat there deeply moved, muttering to myself, "Behold the kindness and sternness of the judge," but I was thinking of God really. As lawbreakers we stand before Him who is sworn to uphold His righteousness. God's instructions on keeping the law are not enough. We lack the means to bring ourselves into compliance. But because of His loving-kindness, God made a way for His mercy to be *justly* given to sinners who would otherwise deserve eternal deportation from His kingdom. He sent His own Son to do the work that we could not do, to meet the just requirements of the law, and He did so *pro bono*, free of charge.

WHO IS JESUS?

Next on our journey from guilt to gladness is discovering who Jesus is, as the One sent by God. The Bible reveals Him to be the miracle we were hoping for. This is evident right from the beginning. The name Jesus literally means "rescuer" or "savior." The angel of the Lord instructed Mary about the miracle in her womb, "You are to give Him the name Jesus, because He will save His people from their sins" (Matthew 1:21).

From the four portraits of Jesus in the Gospels we can summarize His rescue mission as accomplishing two great things at once: He is fulfilling all of God's promises to pardon, reconcile, and transform our lives so that we can live a life pleasing to Him; and He is fulfilling all our hopes for freedom, a clean conscience, and long-term happiness. Put together, Jesus is the fulfillment of all of God's glorious promises to us who put our hope in Him. Notice how the two come together in 2 Corinthians 1:20: "No matter how many promises God has made, they are 'Yes' in Christ. And so through Him the 'Amen' is spoken by us to the glory of God." Through Jesus, God says *yes* to all His promises and we shout *amen* in our new joy. Jesus is the God-sent gift we are hoping for.

OUR EARLIEST DISCOVERIES OF JESUS AS RESCUER

The first glimpse we get of Jesus as our great Rescuer comes from the Old Testament prophecies about Him.[1] Though the promise "I will provide" was given to Abraham, the first clear description of Jesus as the fulfillment of that promise was given to Isaiah centuries later. He wrote, "The virgin will be with child and will give birth to a son, and will call Him Immanuel" (7:14). Immanuel means "God with us" in Hebrew. God, our only hope and rescue, would enter into the human experience, through a virgin, as a baby. Isaiah 9:6 tells us more about this child.

> For unto us a child is born,
>> to us a son is given,
>> and the government will be on His shoulders.

And He will be called
Wonderful Counselor, Mighty God,
Everlasting Father, Prince of Peace.

A son, yet Everlasting Father? A child, yet Mighty God? Mysterious? Yes. Wonderful? No doubt. This fully God, fully man Rescuer is henceforth called by a variety of names: the Messiah (John 1:41), the Anointed One (Daniel 9:25), the Redeemer (Isaiah 59:20), and the Hope of Israel (Jeremiah 14:8). His name is Jesus because He came to rescue *every* repentant sinner who puts his or her hope in God.[2]

A few people, but only a few, were able to recognize in the birth of Christ the promised Savior described by Isaiah centuries before. Mary and Joseph knew from the miraculous conception and from the angelic announcements surrounding His birth (Matthew 1:20). Simeon, a man who prayerfully studied all the messianic prophecies, and Anna, a woman devoted to God, recognized who Jesus was when He was but an infant (Luke 2:25-40). But God in His wisdom let the revelation of Jesus as our Rescuer unfold slowly. Jesus grew up, learning obedience, maturing, and gaining a self-understanding of His mission.

JESUS WOULD HAVE EATEN
CHINESE FOOD WITH ROBERT

When Jesus was thirty years old, He "went public." After being commissioned in a baptismal service, He started to reveal His nature and purpose in the world as our Rescuer (Luke 3:21-23). One of the first things He did (and you've got to love Him for this) was to befriend those He came to save. He didn't network with the movers and shakers, He befriended the official "sinners"— those society said were bad and who themselves believed it.

While Jesus was having dinner at Levi's house, many tax collectors and "sinners" were eating with Him and His disciples, for there were many who followed Him. When the teachers of the law who were Pharisees saw Him eating

with the "sinners" and tax collectors, they asked His disciples: "Why does He eat with tax collectors and 'sinners'?"
On hearing this, Jesus said to them, "It is not the
healthy who need a doctor, but the sick. I have not come
to call the righteous, but sinners." (Mark 2:15-17)

I suspect Jesus would have eaten Chinese food with guys
like Robert. Robert is a huge man from the Deep South. He's
thirty-three years old going on fifty due to a long history of drug
and alcohol abuse. He speaks atrocious English, has worked
multiple odd jobs, and owns nothing. He's stuck in Boston's
worst neighborhood, lives on disability money, and has a sad
and long story of woundedness and waywardness.

Robert and his girlfriend, Belinda, came to see me and our
staff counselor every week for a time. I'd been sowing a vision
into Robert of being a husband and father and a hard worker
who loves and provides for his family. After all, he and Belinda
had been together for seven years and she was having their first
baby. On their third visit I learned that they were married, but
each to *someone else*. Neither had seen his or her spouse in over
ten years. None of the people involved bothered to file divorce.

In addition, Robert couldn't even read his own name. He
"knows his numbers pretty good," he said to me, but not his
letters. Where do I begin to sort this out? No money, no home,
no job, no driver's license, newly sober (but will it last?), a baby
on the way, a family to set up (but how?). Robert is a poor,
messed-up, lost soul. He gets on his knees at the men's shelter
every night and asks God to help him "do good," and since he
can't read it, he sleeps with his Bible under his pillow every night
as a way of showing God he wants to do right.

One week I drove Belinda over to a Christian home for expecting mothers, then I took Robert out for Chinese food. You should
have seen the businessmen turn their heads when I walked in
with Robert in dreadlocks and shabby clothes. I was dressed pretty
sharp that day, and I could tell by the furtive looks that the lunch
crowd was thinking, *Catch a load of these two together!* We sat
there for an hour enjoying hot and sour soup, practicing our

letters, sounding out words, and talking about Jesus. I drove home happy that day, thinking, *Jesus would've enjoyed eating Chinese food with Robert.* He's a lost sinner and he knows it. Jesus loves lost sinners and enjoys their company. "I have not come to call the righteous, but sinners," Jesus said. This is a crucial discovery for those seeking God's forgiveness and reconciliation.

JESUS PARDONED A PARALYTIC

Another discovery we make in surveying the life of Jesus is that He had the authority of God Himself to forgive sinners. Consider His stunning pardon of the paralytic in Mark 2:1-12.

> When Jesus again entered Capernaum, the people heard that He had come home. So many gathered that there was no room left, not even outside the door, and He preached the word to them. Some men came, bringing to Him a paralytic, carried by four of them. Since they could not get him to Jesus because of the crowd, they made an opening in the roof above Jesus and, after digging through it, lowered the mat the paralyzed man was lying on. When Jesus saw their faith, He said to the paralytic, *"Son, your sins are forgiven."*
>
> Now some teachers of the law were sitting there, thinking to themselves, "Why does this fellow talk like that? He's blaspheming! *Who can forgive sins but God alone?"*
>
> Immediately Jesus knew in His spirit that this was what they were thinking in their hearts, and He said to them, "Why are you thinking these things? Which is easier: to say to the paralytic, 'Your sins are forgiven,' or to say, 'Get up, take your mat and walk'? But that you may know that the Son of Man has authority on earth to forgive sins . . . ." He said to the paralytic, "I tell you, get up, take your mat and go home." He got up, took his mat and walked out in full view of them all. This amazed everyone and they praised God, saying, "We have never seen anything like this!"

The disabled man leapt off his mat and started praising God while a bunch of religious professionals went ballistic. "Only God can forgive sins!" they protested. Jesus *agreed*, and that was, of course, the point. He was revealing that He had the fullness of God in Himself; that included the authority to forgive sinners.

Elsewhere He said, "I and the Father are one" (John 10:30). What a remarkable claim! He's asserting that if He forgives you, then God has forgiven you. Later He claimed that it was His forgiveness that we needed to secure our hope in God. "I am the way and the truth and the life. No one comes to the Father except through me" (John 14:6). These striking claims drove the professional clergy nuts because they sounded so blasphemous and arrogant. They failed to consider whether they were true.

The rightness and reasonableness of Jesus making such exclusive claims on our faith can be illustrated by Magalie's experience before the judge. Imagine if Magalie had left the court and called a lawyer *different* from the name the judge gave her, or if she had decided to fill out a sweepstakes form instead of the forms the judge gave her, and sent that in. Would the judge's kindness be honored or demeaned? Would he be angry or thrilled by her creative plan to get right with the law? He said he would be angry if she wavered or delayed in any way. He was willing to work her complete rescue, free of charge, but on one condition: she must trust him *by obeying his instructions*. The apostle Paul calls this "the obedience that comes from faith" (Romans 1:5). Magalie expressed her faith in the judge by calling on *the* lawyer the judge sent her and following his instructions.

So it is with us as we face deportation from God's kingdom. One lawyer has been sent and authorized to pardon our sins and bring us into compliance with the holy law of God. His name is Jesus. All roads do not lead to heaven; one way has been provided. There is no alternate route or plan B. The Jesus Plan rings well with God. "Salvation is found in no one else, for there is no other name under heaven given to men by which we must be saved" (Acts 4:12). We try creative alternatives at our own peril.

THE GREATER OUR GUILT,
THE GREATER OUR RESCUER APPEARS

Another discovery we make of Jesus is that no matter how sinful and guilty we are and feel, Jesus is equal to the task of rescuing and restoring us. In Luke 7:36-50 we read that a Pharisee named Simon had invited Jesus to dinner. Right in the middle of dinner a woman known in the town as a "sinful woman" barged in, carrying "an alabaster jar of perfume, and as she stood behind Him at His feet weeping, she began to wet His feet with her tears. Then she wiped them with her hair, kissed them and poured perfume on them" (37-38). Simon was shocked! "If this man were a prophet, He would know who is touching Him and what kind of woman she is—that she is a sinner," he said to himself (39).

What Simon failed to consider is that God has a heart for great sinners and accepts their confession and desire to be cleansed. He failed to consider that the greatness of God's mercy is revealed in showing mercy to great sinners![3] He failed to consider that if a small debt is forgiven, a small gratitude results. But if a great debt is forgiven, a greater heartfelt joy and thankfulness results. Jesus turned to His host and drove the point home.

> [Jesus] turned toward the woman and said to Simon, "Do you see this woman? I came into your house. You did not give me any water for my feet, but she wet my feet with her tears and wiped them with her hair. You did not give me a kiss, but this woman, from the time I entered, has not stopped kissing my feet. You did not put oil on my head, but she has poured perfume on my feet. Therefore, I tell you, her many sins have been forgiven—for she loved much. *But he who has been forgiven little loves little.*"
>
> Then Jesus said to her, "Your sins are forgiven."
> (Luke 7:44-48)

Great sinners make great lovers of God when Jesus gets hold of them. They tend to live with such an overwhelming vision of the greatness and kindness of God that they become the salt of the earth. One of the most inspiring people I know is my brother in Christ, Leo. Leo constantly thinks of others. He's a guy who proves Benjamin Franklin's maxim "Well done is better than well said." Leo's not articulate—he can't sing, and he'll never lead a Bible study—but he'll notice the fluorescent bulb is out at our counseling center and go buy a replacement without being asked. He'll notice the broken ceiling fan at the home of a single mom at the church and fix it. He'll take our fatherless boys fishing on a Saturday afternoon. When I thanked Leo for fixing my washing machine recently and tried to pay him, he started mumbling about how good Jesus had been to him and refused payment. When you ask Leo what drives him, he gives a clear answer. He's driven by a clear vision of how much Jesus has rescued him from his former life. To Leo, Jesus is a great Savior. This gladness has turned Leo into a glad servant of other people.

If we are going to move from guilt to gladness, we need a clear vision that Jesus welcomes and rewards repentant sinners who put their faith in Him, no matter how deep and foul their behavior. "Your faith has saved you; go in peace," He said to the woman so greatly burdened by her guilt (Luke 7:50). The greater the guilt, the greater the Forgiver's kindness is displayed. Jesus knows that among all those He rescues, those who've been forgiven much will make the greatest lovers of God.

JESUS TRANSFORMS THE LIVES OF THOSE HE FORGIVES

Jesus is a great Savior not only because He forgives great sinners, but because He saves us from sinful behavior. He *always* changes those He forgives. Matthew 1:21 says Jesus is called Savior because He will save His people *from their sins*—not just from the penalty of their sins, but from the enslaving power of sinning itself. What a cruel joke it would be for God to forgive sinners and leave them habitually sinning. Blaise Pascal wrote in his famous *Pensées*, "It is unworthy of God to unite himself to wretched man, yet it is not unworthy of God to lift man up out of his wretchedness."[4] This is what Jesus does as our Rescuer. Second Timothy 1:9 says

Jesus "saved us and called us to a holy life." To get a true and accurate vision of Christ as our Rescuer, we must see that He rescues us from the heartfelt desire to habitually sin.

We see this in His commissioning of Paul. "I am sending you to them to open their eyes and turn them from darkness to light, and from the power of Satan to God, so that they may receive forgiveness of sins and a place among those who are sanctified by faith in me" (Acts 26:17-18). Can there be any doubt that our Rescuer intends to transform our will-to-sin to a will-not-to-sin? Our rescue would be incomplete without it. Our forgiveness would be subject to ridicule.

Jesus fully expects the life of God to be produced in those who hope for the grace of God. In Luke 13:6-9 He teaches this by way of example.

> "A man had a fig tree, planted in his vineyard, and he went to look for fruit on it, but did not find any. So he said to the man who took care of the vineyard, 'For three years now I've been coming to look for fruit on this fig tree and haven't found any. Cut it down! Why should it use up the soil?'
>
> 'Sir,' the man replied, 'leave it alone for one more year, and I'll dig around it and fertilize it. If it bears fruit next year, fine! If not, then cut it down.'"

God is patient but nonetheless expecting to see the fruit that should come from heartfelt repentance and faith. If there is none, over a long period of time, then we too should question the sincerity of our repentance. But for those who have come to hate their sin and put their hope in God, we can trust that Jesus will not only earn a pardon for us but empower us to live a righteous life. This is another reason we call Him our Rescuer.

JONATHAN EDWARDS' EXCELLENT SAVIOR

There is much more we could say about the life and teaching of Jesus that reveals Him to be our great Rescuer. It's important that we get to know Him and continually discover how great a Savior He is—in fact, it's the next step on our journey. The most winsome description of Jesus I've ever read comes from the famous American Puritan Jonathan Edwards in his sermon "The Excellency of Christ." He asks us to consider what we could ever want in a Savior that isn't found in the person of Jesus Christ:

> What is there that you can desire should be in a Savior, that is not in Christ? What excellency is there wanting? What is there that is great or good; what is there that is venerable or winning; what is there that is adorable or endearing; or what can you think of that would be encouraging, which is not to be found in the person of Christ?
>
> Would you have your Savior to be great and honourable, because you are not willing to be beholden to a mean person? And is not Christ a person honourable enough to be worthy that you should be dependent on Him; is He not a person high enough to be appointed to so honourable a work as your salvation? Would you not only have a Savior of high degree, but would you have Him, notwithstanding His exaltation and dignity, to be made also of low degree, that He might have experience of afflictions and trials, that He might learn by the things that He has suffered, to pity them that suffer and are tempted? And has not Christ been made low enough for you; and has He not suffered enough?
>
> Would you have your Savior to be one who is near to God, so that His meditation might be prevalent with him? And can you desire him to be nearer to God than Christ is, who is His only-begotten Son, of the same essence with the Father? And would you not only have him near to God, but also near to you, that you may have free access to him? And would you have him nearer to you than to be in the same nature, united to you by a spiritual union, so close as to be fitly represented by the union of the wife to the husband, of the branch to the vine, of the member

to the head; yea, so as to be one spirit? For so He will be united to you, if you accept Him. . . . What is there wanting or what would you add if you could, to make Him more fit to be your Savior?[5]

Do you see how Edwards' discovery of the person and life of Jesus has produced a confident trust and genuine love for Jesus Christ? This is the path we must follow. We must learn about Jesus. As we do, we will discover how fit He is to be our Savior and how fitting it is that we should entrust ourselves to Him. Through Him our hopes are fulfilled and God's promises are kept. God rescues us through His appointed Rescuer, Jesus Christ. Or as Paul said, "[God] has rescued us from the dominion of darkness and brought us into the kingdom of the Son He loves, in whom we have redemption, the forgiveness of sins" (Colossians 1:13-14).

»

The Journey from Guilt to Gladness

God's promise to rescue and transform our lives and our hope for such a heart-felt experience find mutual fulfillment through the life of Jesus Christ. The next step from guilt to gladness is discovering how true and excellent is Jesus Christ to be our Rescuer.

Chapter Six

Forgiveness Justified

GRASPING THE TRUTH OF THE CROSS

Shame tears my soul, my body many a wound;
Sharp nails pierce this, but sharper that counfound;
Reproaches, which are free, while I am bound,
Was ever grief like mine?
—GEORGE HERBERT, *THE SACRIFICE*

~

God made Him who had no sin to be sin for us,
so that in Him we might become the righteousness of God.
—2 CORINTHIANS 5:21

Elie Wiesel is a Nobel Peace Prize recipient and a Jewish survivor of Auschwitz, the most horrific death camp of World War II. Dr. Wiesel's life mission has been to bring Nazi war criminals to the bar of justice and to remind the world of the immeasurable evil of the Holocaust. When Dr. Wiesel speaks you can hear the wrenching cries of the innocent in his voice as he honors his people and all mankind by demanding justice and warning us "never again." On January 27, 1995, Dr. Wiesel joined other Jewish survivors of Auschwitz in a ceremony to pay tribute to Hitler's victims on the fiftieth anniversary of Auschwitz's "liberation" by the Russian army. As the group gathered around the remains of the concrete crematorium, Wiesel prayed, "God, merciful God, do not have mercy on murderers of Jewish children. Do not have mercy on those who created this place. Do not forgive the people who murdered here."[1]

How should God answer this prayer? To Dr. Wiesel, a

merciful and loving God must be able to get angry and punish, or He is neither merciful nor just. Dr. Wiesel is right. Justice demands that the murderers of millions of innocent Jewish children be cast into the hottest parts of hell's fire. But now the slope gets slippery. Once it's established that a just God cannot fail to punish the wicked, how will anyone escape? Even victims of sin are perpetrators of sin, and the just wages of sin is death. In spite of this, we know that God has pardoned wicked sinners and we may be confident that some of them are repentant murderers, even of children. How does God justify this? Nothing we have learned so far in our survey of the life of Jesus provides a sufficient answer. God would be wrong to pardon a Nazi war criminal, or any other sinner including me, you, and Dr. Wiesel himself, based on what we've learned *so far* about the life of Christ.

God's answer to Dr. Wiesel and all of us caught in the pincers between a desire for mercy and a love of justice is the cross of Christ. The next step in our journey from guilt to gladness involves understanding clearly the death of Jesus on the cross.

WHY DO WE CALL GOOD FRIDAY *GOOD?*

At a key point in His ministry, Jesus took His twelve disciples aside and said,

> "We are going up to Jerusalem, and everything that is written by the prophets about the Son of Man will be fulfilled. He will be handed over to the Gentiles. They will mock Him, insult Him, spit on Him, flog Him and kill Him. On the third day He will rise again." (Luke 18:31-33)

The disciples didn't get it. They couldn't conceive of a plan in which the One they had pinned their hopes on was going to be murdered. They couldn't grasp any reason or benefit in such a crime. Here was a man feeding the hungry and teaching us how to love. Who would want to kill a miracle worker? Why would God allow it? In their mind, that would mean that the Rescuer needs rescuing. Jesus must be mixed up. How could God *ordain*—that is, intentionally purpose—such a thing? God condemns the shedding of innocent blood (Deuteronomy 21:1-9). How could He then condone it when it comes to the most innocent of all men? On what basis could God *want* Him executed?

In spite of these solid arguments, events regarding Jesus happened just as Jesus predicted—just as the prophet Isaiah foretold centuries before:

> He was despised and rejected by men,
> a man of sorrows, and familiar with suffering.
> Like one from whom men hide their faces
> He was despised, and we esteemed Him not. . . .
>
> He was oppressed and afflicted,
> yet He did not open His mouth;
> He was led like a lamb to the slaughter,
> and as a sheep before her shearers is silent,
> so He did not open His mouth. . . .
> He was assigned a grave with the wicked,
> and with the rich in His death,
> though He had done no violence,
> nor was any deceit in His mouth.
>
> Yet *it was the LORD's will to crush Him and cause Him to suffer.* (53:3,7,9-10)

All four Gospels recount how Jesus was arrested, abandoned by His friends, falsely accused, mocked, spit upon, flogged, pierced with a belittling crown of thorns for claiming to be a king, then crucified. The noted German scholar Dr. Martin Hengel reminds us that "crucifixion was not just any kind of death. It was an utterly offensive affair, 'obscene' in the original sense of the word . . . a punishment in which the caprice and sadism of the executioners were given full rein."[2] It was so torturous, in the slow and painful nature by which death finally came, that only the very worst criminals were subjected to it by Roman law.

Luke 22:42-44 records that the night before His crucifixion, Jesus knelt down and prayed,

"Father, if you are willing, take this cup from me; yet not my will, but yours be done." An angel from heaven appeared to Him and strengthened Him. And being in anguish, He prayed more earnestly, and His sweat was like drops of blood falling to the ground.

He was facing the cruelest death ever invented and suffering it as the worst among wicked men. The weight of the pain and the shame is clear. After His arrest and torture, finally "the soldiers took charge of Jesus. Carrying His own cross, He went out to the place of the Skull (which in Aramaic is called Golgotha). Here they crucified Him" (John 19:16-18). This date in history has come to be called Good Friday.

Why is it called *Good* Friday? It's called Good Friday because, on the cross, God glorified Himself by demonstrating His wrath against guilty sinners *and* by manifesting His love for them *at the same time*. It's called Good Friday because on the cross we see the justice of God maintained *and* the mercy of God obtained. It's called Good Friday because this is the work of God, *when grasped by faith*, that transforms our guilt over sin into a gladness toward God, and causes us to live resolutely to the praise of His glory!

WHY CHRIST HAD TO SUFFER AND DIE

Not only did the prophet Isaiah tell us what was to happen to God's promised Rescuer—how Jesus would suffer rejection, humiliation, and execution under the curse of God—he told us *why*.

Surely He took up *our infirmities*
    and carried *our sorrows*,
yet we considered Him stricken by God,
    smitten by Him, and afflicted.

But He was pierced for *our transgressions*,
    He was crushed for *our iniquities*;
the punishment that brought us peace was upon Him,
    and by His wounds we are healed.
We all, like sheep, have gone astray,
    each of us has turned to his own way;
and the LORD has laid on Him
    the iniquity of us all. (John 53:4-6)

We can understand why powerful men, jealous of the power Jesus demonstrated and the acclamation He generated, might seek to have Jesus humiliated and executed as a criminal. What is harder to grasp is why God would purposely *send* His own beloved Son into the world and subject Him to this humiliation and injustice. God's answer is, "He was pierced for our transgressions, He was crushed for our iniquities." Jesus took our punishment.

Incredibly, many well-meaning but unreflective spiritual teachers have denied that the Cross is about divine punishment at all. They do so because they believe that the idea of an angry God—and that "every violation and disobedience [must receive] its just punishment" (Hebrews 2:2)—is contrary to the love of God. For example, in their book *Forgiveness: A Guide for Prayer*, Jacqueline Syrup Bergan and S. Marie Schwan write,

The death of Jesus is not, as has been commonly assumed by many, the result of an offended God punishing a "stand-in" for sinful humanity. We need to approach the Crucified, and see how much we are loved, to see there the kind of love that would prompt our own willingness to give our life for someone we love. And we can, even within the limitations of human loving, imagine ourselves dying for our spouse, children, friends. What seems impossible is to die for someone else, unknown, unloved. And what seems even more impossible, is that someone would do that for me. This is precisely what Paul says God has done for us in Jesus.[3]

I would agree that the apostle Paul says that out of God's great love for us He died. But this death is not like the examples Bergan and Schwan give. If I see a Mack truck barreling down the street and about to hit my son Elliot, my love for him will compel me to run and push him out of the way, even if that means me getting hit and dying. Great love may even cause me to do this for a stranger. Still greater love may cause me to do this for the thug who just stole my wallet and darts away without looking. Men have dived off bridges to save a drowning man and died in the process. Soldiers have thrown themselves on grenades to save their buddies. These are all great acts of love. But these are *not* good examples of Christ on the cross, because they miss the essential point. The Mack truck, the deadly danger, in this case is God! The grenade He threw Himself on is the death-inflicting explosion of His own wrath. If this is not the case, then what was the danger Jesus rescued us from? If there is no danger, why not just *tell* us He loves us and zip back to heaven? Why did He need to *suffer* and *die* to complete His mission, if we are not in the cross hairs of future suffering and death?

The Cross was not a heroic, impulsive act of self-sacrifice to shield us from an unfortunate accident or a dangerous situation. The Cross was God's *intentional* and *punitive* action. "It was the LORD's will to crush Him and cause Him to suffer," declared Isaiah (53:10). Bergan and Schwan may say, "The death of Jesus is not, as has been commonly assumed by many, the result of an offended God punishing a 'stand-in' for sinful humanity." But Isaiah says it's precisely that!

> He was pierced for our transgressions,
> He was crushed for our iniquities. (53:5)

Lest there be any doubt that this suffering is punitive in nature, Isaiah says, "The punishment that brought us peace was upon Him" (Isaiah 53:5).

It's precisely because it was substitutionary *punishment*, that God declares the cross of Christ to be the highest demonstration of His *love* toward those who repent and put their hope in Him.

"This is love: not that we loved God, but that He loved us and sent His Son as an atoning sacrifice for our sins" (1 John 4:10). God shows us His love by turning His just wrath on Himself, in the person of His Son. "God demonstrates His own love for us in this: While we were still sinners, Christ died for us" (Romans 5:8). On the cross, God vents His righteous wrath and displays His unfathomable love.

GRASPING THE TRUTH OF THE CROSS

The heart of the Christian message has been and always will be that "Christ died for our sins" (1 Corinthians 15:3). But in spite of this, many Christians remain hamstrung by their secret guilt and are living very shallow lives. Why is that? I suspect it's because they have nothing but a shallow understanding of the Cross; and in many cases only a small appetite for learning more. Eyes roll at the mere mention of the words *doctrine* and *theology*. These are verbal sleeping pills for many confessing Christians. Yet at the same time they suffer the insomnia of guilt, anxiety, and powerlessness in their faith. They lack confidence and purpose and wonder why. Could it be that a shallow understanding of the Cross is like an inoculation shot? It prevents us from getting the real thing—a full-blown case of sin-uprooting, praise-inspiring, life-altering faith in Christ based on the radical implications of His death on the cross.

First Corinthians 14:20 commands us to "stop thinking like children. In regard to evil be infants, but in your thinking be adults." That is what we must do. Only a truth-soaked *mind* can reshape our opinions, attitudes, responses, and decisions. This is the awesome implication of Jesus' words, "If you hold to my teaching, you are really my disciples. Then you will know the truth, and the truth will set you free" (John 8:31-32). Seismic change is triggered by seismic truths gripped by faith. Therefore I am going to say more about the Cross in hopes that your appetite is growing, not shrinking.

In believing that Christ died for our sins, we are taking a firm grip on two life-liberating truths at work in the Cross. The first is that Christ died for *all* our sins. First John 1:7 says, "If we walk in the light, as He is in the light, we have fellowship with one another, and the blood of Jesus, His Son, purifies us from all sin." What good would it be if Christ paid the penalty for half of my sins? What good would it be if He died for all but one, if that sin deserves an eternal punishment? When I put my hope in Christ, I am receiving by faith that Christ's substitutionary, self-sacrificing death covered over *all* my offenses, so that nothing remains to hinder God's pure love being poured out on me.

The second liberating truth that faith grips dearly is that Christ suffered the *full* punishment justly due for *each* of our sins. Each offense is fully and completely dealt with. We trust that "if we confess our sins, He is faithful and just and will forgive us our sins and purify us from all unrighteousness" (1 John 1:9). This means that anything that would leave a stain of guilt upon us, the smallest mark of unrighteousness, is punished and purged away through the atoning blood of Jesus.

Why is this so liberating for us who believe? Because it means that God is *right* to pardon and restore us to Himself and would be *wrong* not to do so. Isn't that amazing! But think about it. If my sins are fully punished on the cross, and yet I am punished with hell, then my crimes have been punished twice! But the law of justice that demands that I be punished for my crimes, also *protects* me from being punished twice for the same crimes. Justice will not allow it. All the righteous requirements of God's moral law regarding my sin have been carried out on the cross. This is the point made in Romans 8:3-4: "[God] condemned sin in sinful man, in order that the righteous requirements of the law might be fully met in us." The result is that nothing sinful and unpunished now hinders the free flow of God's love toward those who put their faith in Christ. He is justified to show mercy, and with mercy, to give us everything we need to live a life pleasing to Him.

GOD'S REPLY TO A COLLECT CALL FROM PRISON

A few years ago I received a collect call from prison. It was from a man I had met some weeks earlier in the projects, not more than four blocks from my house. This young man struck me as something of a scammer. He was brash and cocky, talking big plans but clearly without a bright future. I liked him immediately. I told him I was a pastor and later I even sent him a little note. Now he was calling me *collect* from the state penitentiary. He was serving a three-to-five-year sentence—for rape! He told me my note was the first personal letter he ever received in his whole life. He asked if I would write a letter for him to the judge. I countered with an offer to visit him instead.

It's sad to think of a child growing up so unloved as to never receive a birthday card or a valentine. This young man was fatherless and his mother was an alcoholic. Sitting in that cell was a wounded young man. But he was also wayward. I didn't want to be scammed. To rape a woman is an immeasurably wicked act of violence and an affront to a just and caring God. Rapists *deserve* jail. Justice demands it. I cared about this young man, but I needed to care also about the well-being of the women in my neighborhood.

If it weren't for the Cross, I wouldn't have known what to say. But here is what I did try to communicate to him over a series of visits (later he was released and I lost track of him). I told him that God is a God of love, and therefore a God of mercy and forgiveness. But I told him first that God is a God of holiness, that He loves righteousness and is angry at him for the harm he did and the harm caused by all his sins. I assured him that God can show mercy to him, but not until he sees how wicked and evil his action is and how much he deserves to be punished.

I didn't say, "Hey, God loves you, so let's just forget that you forced yourself on that young girl, and how much pain and terror you brought her." I said in effect, "If you agree with your accuser and admit that you did evil and deserve to be punished by God, and if you turn to Him who is rightly angry and ask Him for mercy, then you will find that He is able to forgive you. How so? Because God calculated the full amount of punishment needed to vindicate the young woman's dignity, and He calculated the punishment needed to repair the glory of God defaced by your wickedness. Then He totaled it all up and inflicted the full punishment, in righteous anger, on Jesus Christ on the cross. And if you will entrust your life to the living Christ and obey Him, trusting that the Cross is sufficient payment for your sins, God will credit it as your own and redeem your life."

GOD'S ANSWER TO THE PRAYER OF ELIE WIESEL

We can also hazard a guess now as to how God might answer Elie Wiesel's prayer. Remember, he prayed, "God, merciful God, do not have mercy on murderers of Jewish children." God's answer is the Cross. I think He would say something like, "Elie, your passion for justice does you credit. I am committed to always acting justly and ensuring that justice is carried out. My love of justice will ensure that all sinners, from the least to the greatest, from your life even down to the murderers of Jewish children, are punished. For the impenitent, 'blackest darkness is reserved for them' (2 Peter 2:17) in the fires of hell. For the penitent who put their hope in Me, their full punishment has been meted out through the fiery wrath and terrible punishment that I poured out on My beloved Son.[4] Therefore, consider how great is My work on the cross of Christ and put your trust in Me."

The reason we can be sure that God's answer would follow this line is because Romans 3:25-26 affirms that the Cross is a *demonstration* of God's commitment to uphold justice, insuring that even His mercy toward those who trust Him is justifiable. "He did this to *demonstrate His justice*, because in His forbearance He had left the sins committed beforehand unpunished—He did it to demonstrate His justice at the present time, so as to be just and the one who justifies those who have faith in Jesus."

Before the Cross, God's forgiveness of even people like Abraham, Moses, and David *appeared to be unjust*. After all, they were pardoned and no punishment was meted out. Imagine what Uriah thought when he saw David joyously welcomed into the kingdom of God. David seduced his wife, betrayed him with a smile, and murdered him. Might he not call God's justice into question, too? If he did, he was probably told to wait and watch. God would justify His mercy toward David in due time.

When the time came God sent Christ to the cross to justify the mercy He had shown David centuries earlier and to show that, indeed, David's sins did not go unpunished. David and Uriah could love each other as brothers in the kingdom of heaven because Uriah knew that in time God would vindicate him, in righteous wrath. And David knew that in time, God would provide a substitute punishment for his wickedness. Both knew that God's justice would be upheld, even as mercy was extended.

HOW CAN WE KNOW SUCH GOOD NEWS IS TRUE?

Do you see now why the Christian message is called the good news? But is it too good? How do we know it is true? We know because Acts 17:31 says God "has given proof of this [plan of salvation] to all men by raising [Jesus] from the dead." The resurrection of Jesus Christ is God's *validation* that all that Christ did on our behalf—namely, justifying and reconciling us to God—was acceptable and pleasing to God.

The Resurrection *validated* that Jesus was Himself *sinless* and that He died for *our* sins, just as He said. Acts 2:24 says, "God raised [Jesus] from the dead, freeing Him from the agony of death, because it was impossible for death to keep its hold on Him." Why did the justice of God make it impossible for Jesus to stay dead? Because Jesus lived a perfectly righteous life of faithful obedience to the God of all glory, so that death, as a just punishment, had no crime against God to pin itself to (see Psalm 16:8-11). On the streets of Boston, the kids salute the law of justice by saying, "If you can't do the time, don't do the crime." In the case of Jesus, the voice of justice says, "He can't do the time, 'cause He did no crime."

The Resurrection assures us that when Jesus claimed to be God's promised Rescuer and when He claimed to have the divine authority to forgive repentant sinners who put their trust in Him, He spoke the truth. If He was lying, He would not be sitting at the right hand of God but suffering the penalty due Him for deceiving millions of people into trusting a false messiah. The Resurrection is God's stamp of approval on Jesus' claim to be our Lord and Savior.

The Resurrection also sharply defines what it must mean to have faith in Christ. *Because* Christ has been raised from the dead, we are not putting our faith in merely a historical event, but in a living, death-conquering, and reigning Savior. Our faith is *based* on something in the past, but it's *placed* in One who is very much alive today. Notice how the apostle Paul speaks of faith in terms of a living Christ: "I have been crucified with Christ and I no longer live, but Christ lives in me. The life I live in the body, I live by faith in the Son of God, who loved me and gave himself for me" (Galatians 2:20). Paul is living by faith in the living Christ. In Ephesians 3:12 he says this experience is the Christian norm. "In [Christ] and through faith in Him we may approach God with freedom and confidence." Faith connects us to the benefits of the Cross by connecting us to a living Lord. Paul prays that we would experience faith in this way. "I pray that out of His glorious riches He may strengthen you with power through His Spirit in your inner being, so that Christ may dwell in your hearts through faith" (Ephesians 3:16-17).

HOW DO WE LIVE BY FAITH?

What kind of faith so connects us to Christ that He is able to live in our hearts? How do I live by this faith? Our anchor text points the way. Let's look again. "Now He has *reconciled* you by Christ's physical body through death to present you holy in His sight, without blemish and free from accusation—if you continue in your *faith, established and firm, not moved from the hope held out in the gospel*" (Colossians 1:22-23). The kind of faith that connects us to Christ is dependent, persevering, and hope-filled.

Saving faith requires a sense of dependence on the strength, wisdom, and integrity of another. I have saving faith when I yield to the ambulance crew following an accident. In the present case we are depending on Christ. Another word for this is *trust.* I trust you when I am entrusting something to you and depending on you for it. To believe in somebody means the same. Biblically these words (*faith, trust, believe*) are interchangeable. The word most broadly misunderstood is the word *believe.* In the survey that asks, "Do you believe in God?" the answer is nearly always "Yes." People say "I believe," meaning they accept certain doctrinal or religious ideas to be true. This is not saving faith because nothing is at risk, nothing is entrusted, nothing hangs in the balance. Even demons are said to believe in God in the noncommittal sense of acknowledging His existence or attributes (see James 2:19). They would gladly like to believe that "Jesus died for my sins" if that were all faith required.

Someone once illustrated the difference between vain belief and the notion of dependence imbedded in the biblical use of the word *believe* like this. A man was about to walk across a tightrope strung across the raging Niagara Falls. "Do you believe I can do it?" he shouted. Many in the crowd cheered him on, saying, "I believe!" Then he shouted, "The one who believes, come sit on my shoulders." The Bible uses the word *believe* in the latter sense, not the former. We are entrusting our life to Christ.

Saving faith also has a persevering quality to it.[5] I may put my faith in God at some decisive and memorable moment, but inherent in the act is a commitment to be faithful all my life. I must persevere in my commitment before I can fully say I was faithful. I did the same thing in my marriage. At a decisive moment, June 10, 1978, at 4:30 in the afternoon, I gave my life to my wife. But what I gave her in faith was a promise to love her faithfully. The true meaning of the word *faithfully* becomes evident by the fact that I can substitute it for the words *all my days.* "I promise to love you, Kristen, all my days!" The word *faithfulness* makes no sense if persevering, lifelong trust is not inherent in it. That's why Paul says you are reconciled "if you *continue* in your faith . . . *not moved* from the hope of the gospel."

In addition, faith is hope-filled. Faith looks to the past work of Christ on the cross and calculates, "If God did all that for me when I was still alienated from Him by my persistent defiance

and defacement of His glory, how much more can I trust Him
to meet my needs as His beloved child?" Paul reasoned,

> Since we have now been justified by [Christ's] blood, how
> much more shall we be saved from God's wrath through
> Him! For if, when we were God's enemies, we were recon-
> ciled to Him through the death of His Son, how much
> more, having been reconciled, shall we be saved through
> His life! (Romans 5:9-10)

Therefore in looking to God for the forgiveness of our sins, we
are looking to God for everything we will need to make us truly
happy in the long run.

WHY DOES GOD WANT EVERYTHING
TO FLOW THROUGH FAITH?

The reason God wants all His benefits to flow to us through our
faith in Christ is because the alternative method would be to
have us earn them like we earn a paycheck. Why does God consider this bad? After all, if we want a nice car, don't we have to
work hard to pay for it? If I want a beautiful house, don't I have
to pay for it? If things are given to me, don't I in fact value them
less than if I earned them by the sweat of my brow? This is true.

Nevertheless, God's forgiveness doesn't come as an earned
income credit. "For it is by grace you have been saved, through
faith—and this not from yourselves, it is the gift of God—not
by works, so that no one can boast" (Ephesians 2:8-9).

Why does God's grace come by faith alone? To insure that
it's seen by all as the gift of God! A paycheck can never be a present. In order to protect the gift-like quality of His grace, He
commands us to receive it *freely*, through faith alone. After all,
there is a lot more joy in giving a gift than in meeting a payroll,
and God *delights* in being a giver of good gifts.

When my son Nathanael turned fifteen, we bought him a
new, adult-size bike. This kind of gift is highly unusual for us,
so I was excited about the surprise it would be for him. My

satisfaction as the gift giver is the joy of seeing his face light up with joy. He was delighted to receive it and I was delighted to give it. The same is true with our redemption.

I would not have felt more honored if Nathanael had said, "Gee, Pop, this is great, and I promise you I won't ride it until I have taken the garbage out for a month without being asked." I'd be pleased to see him do that, for sure, but not as a *payment* for the bike. I'd be disappointed if he felt he needed to pay for my gift. Then it's no longer a gift! I'd be saddened as well, because given the rate at which teens forget things, he probably would never be able to ride his bike. It would also say something about our relationship that I don't like. I'm his father, not his employer. My joy is in his "Wow!" So it is with God and His gift. His reward as a gift giver is in the gladness of heart that we experience in receiving His gift *as a gift*.

Another reason we can't pay for our sins by doing various good works as a tradeoff for God's mercy is so that no one can boast. "For it is by grace you have been saved, through faith— and this not from yourselves, it is the gift of God—not by works, *so that no one can boast*." Anything we do with a motive of adding to the work of Christ so as to win the forgiveness of God becomes the ground of self-satisfaction in our own goodness, rather than trust in God's grace. If my son earns a bike, he has himself to be proud of. Every bike previous to this one he did earn and purchase on his own. This was good and I was proud of him. In giving him this bike, I wanted to communicate something different, something of my joy in him as my son. He lost all boasting privileges, other than the boast of having a father who loves him and knows how to give good gifts. Among the forgiven there is no boasting either, no sense of having earned anything—only the unending praise for so great a gift, secured at so great a cost and given so freely by the God of all love.

THE SOUL ON ITS KNEES

A saying often attributed to Victor Hugo is that, "There are moments when, whatever the posture of the body, the soul is on its knees." Before the cross of Christ is one of those moments. Archimedes, with his lever in hand, boasted, "give me where to stand and I will move the earth."[6] But Jesus Christ, with His shoulder to the cross, moved something immeasurably harder. He moved heaven's judgment from its course and directed it to Himself, absorbing it all until every evil in us that justified the wrath of God was fully punished. He did this so that His Father's blazing love could freely, abundantly, and righteously flow toward those who put their faith in Jesus Christ.

ॐ

The Journey from Guilt to Gladness

The transformation of guilt into gladness
hastens when we entrust our lives to the
living Christ based on the complete punishment
He suffered in our place on the cross.

Chapter Seven

Forgiveness Experienced

CLEANSING A STAINED CONSCIENCE

A peace above all earthly dignities, a still and quiet conscience.
—SHAKESPEARE, HENRY VIII

෴

Let us draw near to God with a sincere heart in full assurance of faith,
having our hearts sprinkled to cleanse us from a guilty conscience.
—HEBREWS 10:22

The washing away of shame and guilt[1] is properly the *experience* of forgiveness that accompanies our faith in Christ.

When Nana and three of her friends came to see me, our conversation reminded me how awesome and immediate the cleansing power of the gospel is when gripped by faith. In the previous months our center helped Nana through her pregnancy. One thing that helped her find strength was the pictures she saw of a preborn child. The other was the relationship counseling we provided for her and her partner of eleven years. Things improved so much that a month before the baby was born, I was pleased and honored to conduct their wedding.

On this day Nana brought her friends in to show them the beautiful Lennart Nilsson pictures made famous in *Life Magazine*. They reveal the beauty of a baby growing in the womb. As the women passed the pictures around excitedly, one of them turned to me. A solitary tear dripped down her cheek as she said, "I had an abortion two years ago and now it hurts so bad in my heart. Is there anything I can do?"

Before I could answer, another of Nana's friends said, "Oh yes. You can fast. Fasting will help a lot." Nana agreed quickly that fasting might help relieve her guilt. In their way of thinking, past wrong behavior is counterbalanced with good behavior or self-punishing behavior. In this case they were hoping that fasting would pay down on the debt of guilt she felt and cause her to feel better.

I smiled and turned to Nana's friend. "Dear, fasting is a good thing but not in this situation. I doubt, first of all, given how tenderhearted you clearly are, that even if you fasted to the brink of starvation, you would feel any sense of assurance that you had paid *in full* for the guilt you feel in your heart. But I want you to know that God is pleased with your tears and your confession to us. What you did was wrong. God is angered whenever children are killed intentionally. But because God wanted to show you His great love, He sent Jesus Christ into the world to suffer the full punishment due all your sins. Christ did this by dying on the cross. After which God raised Him up again. You honor Him best, not by fasting, but by trusting in Christ for the forgiveness of your sins and for everything else necessary to please God with your life. This means believing that the terrible suffering Christ endured on your behalf is sufficient for even the death of your baby."

Nana's friend looked up, and another tear fell from her eye. "That is the most beautiful story I have ever heard," she replied. It was the word *beautiful* in her response that indicated to me that she had heard the gospel in her heart. It showed me again that believing is cleansing!

CHRIST DIED TO CLEANSE OUR CONSCIENCE

When Christ went to the cross, He died to clear not only the path for God's mercy but also the path for our conscience to be purified. God wills that we experience His mercy as a clean conscience. Listen to how emphatically Hebrews 9:14 stresses this point: "How much more, then, will the blood of Christ, who through the eternal Spirit offered himself unblemished to God, *cleanse our consciences* from acts that lead to death, so that we may serve the living God!" Just as our faith in the blood of Christ removes God's condemnation, so our faith in Christ should remove our self-condemnation. The cleansing agent is the blood of Christ. It's activated by faith. The apostle Peter says Christ was "put to death in the body . . . [as a] pledge of a good conscience toward God" (1 Peter 3:18,21). This pledge was *secured* on the cross and is *made good* by the power of the Spirit at work in our *faith* (1 Peter 3:18). I could see it beginning to work in Nana's friend. She was embracing the truth of the gospel and immediately experiencing a heartfelt relief.

The Bible reveals that Christ died to remove our *shame* as well as our sin. Shame is the emotional pain we feel over past sinful behavior. Shame can be imposed on us, too. We can be *put to shame* when our sin is known by others. Their contempt is our shame. But Christ bore all our shame as well as our guilt. Hebrews 12:2 says He "endured the cross, scorning its shame." He willingly died in such a way as to suffer great contempt, degradation, and humiliation. Therefore, "the one who trusts in Him will never be put to shame" (Romans 9:33).

Still another way the Bible expresses our experience of God's forgiveness is to speak of our *peace* with God. Romans 5:1-2 says, "Since we have been justified through faith, we have peace with God through our Lord Jesus Christ, through whom we have gained access by faith into this grace in which we now stand." Though we were once enemies, God has made His peace with us through Christ. Therefore, by faith we ought to also enjoy *peace of mind*, disregard our past sins, and approach God confidently. We are at peace. On this we must stand.

If we don't, a stained conscience will definitely keep us from experiencing God's forgiveness. Without this experience we won't feel confidence about our relationship with God on any other matter. So it's imperative that we bring our consciences to God *by faith* for a good soaking in the cleansing blood of Christ. Hebrews 10:22 says, "Let us draw near to God with a sincere heart in full assurance of faith, having our hearts sprinkled to cleanse us from a guilty conscience." Being free to draw near to God is the whole point of God's plan of reconciliation. This requires removing every stain of conscience. I picture this as my faith doing a full inventory of every claim my conscience has filed against me and stamping it "paid in full" with the blood of Jesus. This is my right, privilege, and obligation as a Christian.

If my conscience objects to my confidently drawing near to God to praise or petition Him, then I must be willing to stand on the truth of the gospel and contend for my faith. Conscience shouts, "I object." I reply, "On what basis?" Conscience says, "You did such-and-such. How can you possibly think God doesn't see it?" Faith says, "You have a good point. I will not deny the facts. But I ask, 'Was it or was it not a sin for which Christ died? If yes, was it or was it not paid in full by Him out of His great love for me?'" Our conscience will soon withdraw the objection and agree with us that we ought to draw near to God and say, "Thank You, Father, for paying for that awful sin my conscience has just brought to mind. I rejoice all the more deeply in your lovingkindness." We can truly say, "Therefore, there is now no condemnation for those who are in Christ Jesus" (Romans 8:1). Such is the cleansing power of faith on a stained conscience.

WHAT KEEPS US FROM EXPERIENCING GOD'S FORGIVENESS?

Some things, like dandelions, never seem to go away for good. Shame and guilt can be like that. They constantly reassert themselves and keep us from experiencing the joy of a "good conscience toward God." What makes persistent shame a serious problem is that it belies a *persistent* unbelief in the sufficiency of Christ to atone for our guilt. It calls the truth of the gospel into question. And that is a serious matter.

One way it does that is by constantly interpreting life's hardships as a sign of God's continuing anger for past evil behavior. Persistent shame whispers, "God is punishing me." An amazing example of this is found in Genesis 42. Joseph's brothers, in a fit of jealousy and resentment for the blessing on Joseph's life, sold him into slavery. Then they lied to their father, telling him Joseph was mauled by a wild animal. They kept this wickedness a secret for decades!

Yet, when things went wrong (and don't they always!), the voice of persistent shame hurled condemnation upon them. At one point, Israel was experiencing a famine and the brothers went to buy food from the Egyptians. If you know the story, you know that the Egyptian administrator of grain distribution ends up being Joseph. The brothers negotiated with him for food without any idea whom they were talking to. When things went bad in the process, one of the brothers interpreted their trouble, saying, "Surely we are being punished because of our brother. We saw how distressed he was when he pleaded with us for his life, but we would not listen; that's why this distress has come upon us" (Genesis 42:21). This is decades after they got rid of their brother! Their experience shows us how certain things committed forty or fifty years ago can still persistently gnaw away at us.

One reason is obvious. Like the brothers of Joseph, we've still never come clean. We've never repented. We merely lop off our guilt like we mow down dandelions. As soon as we don't see it, we think it's not there. After a season, the thing pops up again and we lop it off again. In this mode, we'll never get relief because we're really back at the starting point of admitting our guilt.

However, sometimes the problem is due to an oversensitive conscience and a serious fault in our understanding of God — in other words, bad theology! A friend who suffered a house fire confided to me once, "I think God was punishing me for not doing the things I should be doing as a Christian." I was so grieved to hear this. God does *discipline* those He loves, but He *punishes* those He loves not by burning their house down, but by sending His Son into the world to suffer our due punishment on the cross. Her comment reflects a serious defect in her faith. She will never experience the full assurance of God's lovingkindness if she thinks God burned her house down for poor devotional habits. God is grieved that we should think Him so quick-tempered and irrational.

Yet, because sin has warped our thinking about who God is, it's natural for us to play connect-the-dots when things go wrong. When my oldest son, Nathanael, was only six and still new at riding a bike, one day he fell off and scraped his knee. Earlier that day I had disciplined him for some minor offense and had already forgotten about it. Nathanael had not. As I wiped away his tears and tended to his bleeding knee, he looked up and said, "I think God let me fall off my bike because of what I did this morning."

In reply I said, "No, Son, He did not. He let you fall off your bike so that you would learn to overcome hardships and develop a persevering character. God loves that.[2] When God wants to send a message that you've done something wrong, He doesn't send you a bike accident, He sends you your mom and me to tell you directly and clearly. You don't have to guess. When He wanted to *punish* you for your sins, He sent His own Son to die on the cross as your substitute punishment. Understand?"

That may sound like a lot of theology for a lad of six, but in fact it made good sense to him. He was relieved. He loved me for saying it. He got up on his bike and tried again.

If God is punishing us through the hardships of life, then the Cross cannot be our complete atonement,[3] and the apostle Paul overstated the case when he said, "There is now no condemnation for those who are in Christ Jesus." Some lingering judgment must be causing bad things to happen. But the truth is, "since we have the forgiveness of sins and God is no longer our enemy but our Father, we can allow His peace to rule in our hearts experientially, *despite life's sufferings*" (Romans 5:1).[4]

THE INABILITY TO FORGIVE OURSELVES

A second way persistent shame expresses itself is in the words "I know God forgives me, but I just can't forgive myself." Hearing this also pains me, and as a Christian counselor I hear it often. I understand that when we first begin to grasp the enormity of our guilt, and before we've had a chance to grasp the extent of Christ's sufferings, we should be angry with ourselves and think that we ought not forgive ourselves even if God does. This would be the voice of immature faith, not unbelief. It's the spiritual equivalent of living through that awful Saturday between Good Friday and Easter morning. One truth is clear, the full truth is still a day away. Even so, any attempt to live the Christian life in the Saturday mode is doomed to fail. Christ is risen.

In the books I've read on guilt, heavy emphasis is placed on the need to forgive yourself, more so even than on the need to know that God forgives you. Usually a number of steps are given to help people forgive themselves. I'm not persuaded that this is a biblical method for defeating persistent shame. It's quite possible God is insulted by it. I know this may sound harsh, if not shocking, but bear with me. If we admit that God forgives us but we don't forgive ourselves, are we not insulting His judgment and exalting our own, as if we have a higher standard of justice than He does?

The reason we don't see this at first is because humility is a Christian virtue, and to say "I know that God forgives me but I can't forgive myself" sounds humble. But beneath the surface we are apt to find a fiercely proud sense of having better judgment than God.[5] The very question of *self*-forgiveness may reflect a resistance to glory in God's mercy and a preference to grind our teeth for failing to be as good as our pride always assured us that we were.

One way to silence this voice of self-condemnation is to humbly remind ourselves that the Christian experience of forgiveness makes us God-centered, not self-centered. So the Christian way of thinking is to say, "If God is satisfied, who cares what others think. Even my own judgment ought not to matter. If God has assured me of His mercy, I will exalt in His mercy and rest in His judgment." This is precisely what Romans 8:31, 33-35 teaches us to think.

> If God is for us, who can be against us? . . . Who will bring any charge against those whom God has chosen? It is God who justifies. Who is he that condemns? Christ

Jesus, who died—more than that, who was raised to life—is at the right hand of God and is also interceding for us. Who shall separate us from the love of Christ?

Here is our victory. Here is the Christian's hope.

√ THE ONLY UNFORGIVABLE SIN

When we allow ourselves to shift our concern from God's judgment to our own, not only do we exalt our judgment above God's, but we belittle the entire work of Christ. In effect we're saying, "It's not good enough." Such a state of mind is not tolerated in the Bible. Indeed, the most severe warnings in all the Bible come precisely at that point in which someone challenges the sufficiency and effectiveness of God's work of forgiveness, reconciliation, and liberation through Jesus Christ. In Matthew 12:31-32, Jesus says sternly,

> "Every sin and blasphemy will be forgiven men, but the blasphemy against the Spirit will not be forgiven. Anyone who speaks a word against the Son of Man will be forgiven, but anyone who speaks against the Holy Spirit will not be forgiven, either in this age or in the age to come."

Admittedly, this is a difficult verse to grasp. What does it mean to "speak against the Holy Spirit"? Taking our cue from the rest of Scripture, we can observe that the entire work of God's forgiveness and reconciliation is attributed to the *work of the Spirit*. Hebrews 9:14 says it was *"through the eternal Spirit* [that Christ] offered himself unblemished to God." First Peter 3:18 says Christ was "made alive *by the Spirit.*" Our belief in the truth and our commitment to trust in Christ is called the "sanctifying work of the Spirit" (1 Peter 1:2, 2 Thessalonians 2:13). Therefore, the one thing God will not tolerate—indeed, the only thing He ultimately refuses to forgive— is the sin of discounting the work of grace wrought by the Spirit of God. This is the unforgivable sin, for it belittles the work of the Cross and calls it insufficient or unnecessary.

Once we've discovered how much Christ suffered in love to justify His mercy toward us, and once we've learned that He rose from the dead to be our living Lord, if we then conclude "Not good enough," we are *unbelievers*. Since *persistent* shame is a form of *persistent* unbelief in the sufficiency of the Cross, this warning applies as well:

> If we deliberately keep on sinning after we have received the knowledge of the truth, no sacrifice for sins is left, but only a fearful expectation of judgment and of raging fire that will consume the enemies of God. Anyone who rejected the law of Moses died without mercy on the testimony of two or three witnesses. How much more severely do you think a man deserves to be punished who has trampled the Son of God under foot, who has treated as an unholy thing the blood of the covenant that sanctified him, and who has insulted *the Spirit of grace?* . . . So do not throw away your confidence. (Hebrews 10:26-29,35)

To "insult the Spirit of grace" echoes the earlier warning against "blasphemy against the Spirit." The point is that if we are to be afraid of anything, or ashamed of anything, it shouldn't be the evil behavior in our past, but rather our *present unbelief* that we could look at the suffering of Christ and think it not good enough to cleanse us from *all* unrighteousness and reconcile us to God. Remember this when battling against the guilt of particularly selfish, gross, or violent sins. Christ agrees that our sin is damnable, but because of His great love for us He suffered the *full* penalty due for all and each of our damnable acts. We must meet persistent shame with persistent faith in the sufficiency of Christ for our salvation.

SHOULD CHRISTIANS EVER FEEL ASHAMED?

It's good to make a distinction between things that happened long ago that have been set right, as far as is possible, and things that we do in the ongoing struggle against sin that we have persistently refused to admit responsibility for. In the first, we honor God by accepting the cleansing of our consciences. In the latter, we honor God by being ashamed of ourselves and turning from it by the grace of God.

Even though King David was assured of forgiveness, he still wrote Psalm 51 expressing his shame and sorrow over his sin. He confessed to doing "evil in [God's] sight" (verse 4). I'm happily married, but that doesn't mean I'm never sad or angry at myself for saying or doing things that hurt my wife. My ability to sorrow or feel ashamed is one reason I can maintain a long-term, happy relationship with her, and she with me.

When our problem is not persistent unwarranted shame over things long forgiven but rather a persistent sinful habit not yet faced, shame has a medicinal value. It's a necessary inducement to true repentance. Paul used it on one occasion. Regarding an obstinate brother he recommended, "Do not associate with him, in order that he may feel ashamed. Yet do not regard him as an enemy, but warn him as a brother" (2 Thessalonians 3:14-15).

Second Corinthians 7:11, a paradigm for true repentance, shows us the proper role of shame in our lives. "See what this godly sorrow has produced in you: what earnestness, what eagerness to clear yourselves, what indignation, what alarm, what longing, what concern, what readiness to see justice done." Until I permit myself the *short-term* painful experience of shame or self-loathing, until I hate what demeans God's glory and hurts others, my heart will never be converted and I'll never have the strength to change.

A friend of mine is a crack addict. He repents and weeps repeatedly. But what has always been lacking in his tears, and has always made his repentance false and ineffective, is a true and deep godly sorrow and sense of shame for all the lying and stealing and abuse involved in his addiction. He's sorry that he got caught. He's not sorry that he's hooked. He's embarrassed before his wife and sons, but he's not alarmed, indignant, ready to wage a war against an enemy out to kill him and his family. He's not sick of his sin. He's only sick of the consequences. He needs the medicine of shame. Unfortunately, none of the many rehab programs he's been in induce shame. They think the problem is low self-esteem and that it would be shameful to tell him to be ashamed of himself. But there is such a thing as a healthy shame that leads to a healthy zeal to overcome a habitual sin. A healthy fear of God produces a healthy hatred for sin.

STRIVING FOR A GOOD CONSCIENCE

Shakespeare called the quiet conscience "a peace above all dignities." A peaceful conscience makes for bold prayers, passionate praise, confident service, courageous suffering for the sake of righteousness. It makes for healthier long-term relationships and sound sleeping. But when we lose our peace, and we all do, then we must be prepared to humble ourselves before our gracious God. The loss of peace signals the need for self-inspection and action. In learning to live by a clear conscience, we must learn to follow a few of God's guiding principles. Among them are:

1. Allow a season of sorrow for sin. It's godly sorrow. It leads to the actions of repentance. It means my conscience is working. We do well to consider the shame of bad behavior.

2. Rest in the truth of the gospel. It's a special foretaste of hell to be convicted of the evil of sin without trusting in the righteousness of Christ's sacrifice for sin. A good conscience weeps for a short time, then comes to rest again in the gift of God in Jesus Christ. In this way shame spurs change but doesn't become persistent or disabling or demeaning to the work of Christ. We must trust Christ as both "the author and *perfecter* of our faith" (Hebrews 12:2).

3. Restore what is restorable. Part of what it means to repent and believe is to return any benefit that sin has provided us and trust in Christ instead. Sin, after all, does provide fleeting pleasures. In renouncing it, it's important that we not continue to benefit from it. Therefore restoration is part of repentance (see Luke 19:1-10). For example, if I have embezzled from the company because I didn't trust in God's provision for me, repentance, faith, and my desire for a clean conscience will compel me to return the money. It may also ask me to pay a fine to ensure that the pain of sin consciously outweighs the pleasure of sin. If I am afraid of the consequences, then I will still return the money; it's just that now I will learn the discipline of daily prayer. I will learn how much Christ can be trusted with my life. Making restitution where possible cleanses the conscience.

4. *Remember that God forgets.* In striving for a good conscience, remember that God forgets. In Jeremiah 31:33-34, the Lord instituted a covenant with His people:

"For I will forgive their wickedness
and will remember their sins no more."

The word *remember* is not used in a cognitive sense. God is omniscient, after all. It's used in a relational sense that He will not hold our sins up to us as a barrier to our ongoing fellowship with Him. In this sense He renders them forgotten. He removes our sin and shame and deposits them into the deepest part of the sea. "There," as Corrie ten Boom once said in her wise and childlike way, "He posts a sign, 'No fishing allowed.'"[6] In striving for a good conscience we need to remember to forget.

5. *Endure hardship as God's discipline, not damnation.* We experience the conviction of God as He fashions us into His holiness and likeness, but there is no condemnation. Hebrews 12:7,10-11 reminds us of the distinction:

Endure hardship as discipline; God is treating you as sons. . . . Our fathers disciplined us for a little while as they thought best; but God disciplines us for our good, that we may share in His holiness. No discipline seems pleasant at the time, but painful. Later on, however, it produces a harvest of righteousness and peace for those who have been trained by it.

6. *Bear your scars graciously.* It is no small lesson that the risen Lord, utterly transformed in His glorified body, still maintained His nail scars! They remain as a testimony to the grace of God. Scars offer a reminder of a wound. But they also testify

to having been healed. We may choose to hide the scars of our past sin in shame and guilt, or bear them graciously as a testimony to the grace of God. They are our testimony to our need for forgiveness and the sign of having received it. In this way, our triumph over shame is completed. For what guilt and shame once used to blackmail us into silence, God now uses to make our testimony ring authentic and glad of heart. In fighting for a good conscience we must bear our scars as a testimony of God's forgiveness and healing, not as a mark of disqualification.

The Journey from Guilt to Gladness

Experiencing God's forgiveness in the form of a clean conscience moves us another step forward from guilt to gladness. We cleanse our conscience by putting our faith in the sufficiency of Christ and the punishment He endured on our behalf.

Part Three

The Heart
Made Glad

❧

Chapter Eight

Forgiveness Enjoyed

LIVING UNDER THE INFLUENCE OF GRACE

My sin—O the bliss of this glorious thot—
My sin, not in part, but the whole,
Is nailed to the cross, and I bear it no more:
Praise the Lord, praise the Lord, O my soul!
—HORATIO G. SPAFFORD, *IT IS WELL WITH MY SOUL*

᠀

Sing, O Daughter of Zion;
shout aloud, O Israel!
Be glad and rejoice with all your heart,
O Daughter of Jerusalem!
The LORD has taken away your punishment.
—ZEPHANIAH 3:14-15

Dr. Larry Crabb, one of America's leading Christian psychologists, once asked, "What do I need more than anything else to make me deeply happy?" He suggests most people would answer this question with the following:

᠀ a husband who would stop drinking
᠀ a more sexually aroused wife
᠀ a medical report that the tissue is benign
᠀ a better job
᠀ more money
᠀ a man to marry
᠀ an estranged son to come home
᠀ a rebellious daughter to straighten out
᠀ a husband or wife or parent or child to come to Christ[1]

While we would be happy to see any of these painful concerns met, Dr. Crabb suggests that "each of these responses is a wrong answer to the question, What do I need *more than anything else* to make me deeply happy? There is only one correct answer: forgiveness from God that brings me into relationship with Him and ongoing forgiveness that makes continued fellowship possible. Every other answer is wrong."[2]

David got it right:

> Blessed [glad of heart] is he
>> whose transgressions are forgiven,
>> whose sins are covered.
> Blessed is the man
>> whose sin the LORD does not count against him
>> and in whose spirit is no deceit. (Psalm 32:1-2)

When our sins are forgiven and our consciences are cleansed, we are freed up to enjoy God Himself and all that He has for us as the vessels of His mercy. Forgiveness, then, is the foundation of God's work of grace, not the capstone. It's an entry point, not an arrival point, for God's work of grace. We are forgiven in order that we might learn to live, and enjoy living, an upright and holy life in all fear and reverence to God. Learning to live under the continuing influence of God's grace is another step from guilt to gladness.

LIVING UNDER THE INFLUENCE

In 1987, Fred was lying in a hospital bed, so pickled from years of alcoholism that he was near death. The day he drove to the detox center, he had a coffee mug full of Scotch with him and sat in the parking lot gulping it down before checking in. Meanwhile, without his knowledge, his wife, Diane, was scheduled to file divorce papers. She had watched him slide into drunkenness and suffered his abusive language and lying for far too long. The man she once loved, she now hated. He had destroyed their marriage and hurt the children terribly.

Fred lay in his bed with alcoholic hepatitis, liver damage, and bronchial pneumonia. He had lost bowel control, the lining of his stomach was shot, and he was jaundiced. The hospital contacted Diane and warned her to prepare for his death. Fred lay on his bed, shaking with tremors and weeping with remorse. "I felt so ashamed, like such a failure and so alone," he told me. After many hours, perhaps days, of remorse and confession, he began to get a revelation of God's loving-kindness. He first tasted it in 1966 during a time when God was wooing him to faith. He responded initially, but like so many, failed to live under the daily influence of grace, and therefore his faith was ineffective. Lying in his bed, he felt the grace of God wooing him once again, and he resolved to put his hope entirely in the hands of God and repent from ever drinking again. He remembers saying, "If I live, I will serve the Lord."

During the time Fred was going through his godly sorrow and repentance, Diane was receiving biblical counsel from her aunt. As an act of faith in God's Word, which says, "I hate divorce" (Malachi 2:16), she tore up the divorce papers. She made sure Fred got the medical attention he needed. She told Fred of her secret plans to leave him, her decision to stay and why. The Sunday following Fred's dismissal they were together in church. She prayed for Fred's healing. Fred prayed for God to give him the resolve to repair their marriage as far as was possible, and he asked his wife for forgiveness.

The whole church was soon riveted with joy as their story unfolded. Here was a couple headed for divorce—if death didn't get there first. But now they were alive and together before the throne of mercy! Fred never drank again. I can testify that in the ten years since, Fred served the Lord with great compassion. Right before this book went to press, Fred died of cancer. I will always remember him for how he continually confessed his need for the continuing grace of God. He was ever learning to live under the influence of God's grace till his last moments.

Fred's story is not unusual. It follows the biblically revealed course for the normative Christian experience of God's forgiveness. Initially, God's grace spared his life; subsequently, it changed his life. Initially, he experienced God's grace in the forgiveness of his sins; subsequently, he experienced it as a conquering power over sinful habits. Initially, grace saved his marriage; subsequently, it repaired his life as a man, a husband, a father, a laborer, a neighbor, and a citizen.

Fred's transformation illustrates how our desire to be happy and God's desire to be glorified meet in the Christian experience of God's grace. Fred was *glad* to be forgiven, *thankful* to be sober, and *happy* to learn God's will for his life. He enjoyed his new relationship to God, his family, and his local church and was pleased to serve where needed. All this gladness of heart expressed itself in thanksgiving to God. His wife was obviously pleased with the change too, and praised God for it. The whole church rejoiced to see their lives and marriage rescued, so they sang the praises of God. Jesus taught us that all heaven breaks out in radical joy over the work of God's grace.

> "Suppose one of you has a hundred sheep and loses one of them. Does he not leave the ninety-nine in the open country and go after the lost sheep until he finds it? And when he finds it, he joyfully puts it on his shoulders and goes home. Then he calls his friends and neighbors together and says, 'Rejoice with me; I have found my lost sheep.' I tell you that in the same way there will be more rejoicing in heaven over one sinner who repents than over ninety-nine righteous persons who do not need to repent." (Luke 15:4-7)

If the angels of heaven rejoice so freely when one sinner, like Fred, repents, imagine how much joy there is in heaven as thousands of people every day admit their guilt and receive the gift of God's forgiveness and a regenerated life! No wonder heaven resounds with unending praise to God! John Piper wrote,

> God's quest to be glorified and our quest to be satisfied reach their goal in this one experience: our delight in God overflows in praise. For God, praise is the sweet echo of His own excellence in the hearts of His people. For us, praise is the summit of satisfaction that comes from living in fellowship with God.[3]

If true, then the way to experience true and lasting happiness is to walk the straight beam of God's grace till He calls us to Himself.

LEARNING TO LIVE UNDER THE INFLUENCE OF GRACE

Jeremiah 31:31-34 reveals the pathway that God's grace will follow as He continues to work on those He forgives.

> "The time is coming," declares the LORD,
>   "when I will make a new covenant
> with the house of Israel
>   and with the house of Judah. . . .
> *I will put my law in their minds*
>   *and write it on their hearts.*
> I will be their God,
>   and they will be my people.
> No longer will a man teach his neighbor,
>   or a man his brother, saying, 'Know the LORD,'
> because they will all know me,
>   from the least of them to the greatest," declares the LORD.
> "For I will forgive their wickedness
>   and will remember their sins no more."

God calls this promise of continuing grace a new covenant. *Every* recipient of His gift of forgiveness is going to undergo a radical transformation over time. It will not be completed until we are thoroughly glad to live to the praise of His glory. Our minds are going to learn who God is, His power and majesty, along with what pleases and displeases Him. Our hearts are going to undergo reconstruction so that we desire what He desires.

Our former alienation will be replaced with a kindred spirit of friendship as well as devotion. As recipients of the grace of God, we will experience this continuing influence in three heartfelt ways:

- a glad heart to worship God,
- a glad heart to obey God, and
- a joyful assurance of His delight and acceptance of us now and forever.

But before we expand on these three, let me first remove a possible objection or point of confusion.

Is the continuing work of grace God's work or ours? It's hard to speak of God making all these changes in our lives without "hearing" that we are passive in the process. It sounds like human responsibility is being jettisoned. So let me clarify. Even though our holiness is the work of God and not our own, it's *not* a work God does independently of our will and decision-making responsibilities. Jeremiah shows us that where *God* is at work, *my* heart's desire and *my* will are changing.

God clearly appeals to my will even as He transforms it. Jesus called out for Lazarus to rise up (John 11:43), but with the call came the powerful work of grace, raising Lazarus from the dead. Without that attending grace, Lazarus would not even hear the call, let alone heed it. The dynamics are the same for all Christians. Philippians 2:12-13 says, "Therefore, my dear friends, as you have always obeyed . . . continue to work out your salvation with fear and trembling, for it is God who works in you to will and to act according to His good purpose." If I understand this correctly, it means that God is not changing me against my will, nor saving me in spite of my willful disobedience, nor even delivering me from a sinful habit separately from my own resolve to do so. He is saving me by changing my will, giving me a new heart's desire and steering it like a rudder on a ship, so that I desire to live to His honor.

Therefore, it's not surprising to read that God promises to make me righteous while commanding me to do the right thing. God promises, "I will cleanse you from all your impurities and from all your idols. I will give you a new heart and put a new spirit in you; I will remove from you your heart of stone and give you a heart of flesh. And *I will put my Spirit in you and move you to follow my decrees and be careful to keep my laws*" (Ezekiel 36:25-27). Having equipped us with a new heart and His own Spirit of holiness, He directs and commands and warns and urges us to live a holy life. "I urge you to live a life worthy of the calling you have received" (Ephesians 4:1). Where there is resistance on my part, He doesn't hesitate, as a loving Father, to discipline me. Where light alone fails, heat often can succeed. He *teaches* me godliness; He doesn't zap me with a fairy wand and get a zombie for a son. This being the case, let's consider the life-changing power of the Christian experience of God's forgiveness.

A GLAD HEART TO WORSHIP GOD

Once the lyrics of the gospel have been written on our hearts, the melody of the gospel bursts forth as a song of gladness and praise to God. Zephaniah 3:14-15 says,

> Sing, O Daughter of Zion;
> shout aloud, O Israel!
> Be glad and rejoice with all your heart,
> O Daughter of Jerusalem!
> The LORD has taken away your punishment.

This is why the gospel is called "*good* news of great *joy*." In truth, the only way to believe this good news rightly is to believe it gladly.

> Let all who take refuge in you be glad;
> let them ever sing for joy. (Psalm 5:11)

The first evidence of living under the influence of grace is a spontaneous, irresistible, and abiding joy in God that causes us to praise His name. We're like the Munchkins in Oz. When the house fell on the wicked witch, they called to one and all, "Let the joyous news be spread, the wicked old witch at last is dead!" So in our case the fatal blow against our enmity with God has been given. His just anger is fully vented; the just penalty is fully paid; the righteous requirements of the law are fully met in Christ. Our guilt and shame are fully purged, the desire for sin is mortally wounded, God's love is unrestrained, and the Spirit of Christ is dwelling in us as a down payment of heaven itself. We have good reason to rejoice in humble adoration![4] Therefore,

> Let us rejoice and be glad
>> and give Him glory! (Revelation 19:7)

Since our desire to worship God often exceeds our knowledge of how to express ourselves, God has provided us with a book of worship, the book of Psalms, to help us worship Him with a glad heart.

> You make me glad by your deeds, O LORD;
>> I sing for joy at the works of your hands. (Psalm 92:4)

> Then will I go to the altar of God,
>> to God, my joy and my delight.
> I will praise you with the harp,
>> O God, my God. (Psalm 43:4)

> My heart is glad and my tongue rejoices;
>> my body also will rest secure,
> because you will not abandon me to the grave,
>> nor will you let your Holy One see decay.
> You have made known to me the path of life;
>> you will fill me with joy in your presence,
> with eternal pleasures at your right hand. (Psalm 16:9-11)

> Sing to the LORD a new song,
>> for He has done marvelous things. . . .
> Shout for joy to the LORD, all the earth,
>> burst into jubilant song with music. (Psalm 98:1,4)

The Christian church will forever continue to produce new songs of worship and the poetry of praise.

I often find myself repeating Edward Taylor's prayer for God's grace to continue influencing every part of my life, culminating always in my increased joy over God's glorious grace.

Lord, feed mine eyes then with thy doings rare,
    And fat my heart with these ripe fruits thou bear'st
Adorn my life well with thy works; make fair
    My person with apparel thou prepar'st.
My boughs shall loaded be with fruits that spring
Up from thy works, while to thy praise I sing.[5]

A GLAD HEART TO OBEY GOD

Those whom God *declares* righteous, He *makes* righteous; it's also part of the continuing influence of grace and the promise of God.

"I will put my law in their minds
    and write it on their hearts." (Jeremiah 31:33)

The work of righteousness doesn't complete its work in a day. We don't plant lettuce in the morning and expect a salad for supper. The growth of righteousness imitates natural growth. It takes time to show itself, just as the lettuce seed takes time to look like lettuce. But Christians desire to grow up into a reflection of Christ to the honor of Christ, or they are not Christians. The grace that pardons *always* purifies.

Why can I say this so absolutely? Because Titus 2:11-12 says the grace of God that brings salvation always produces Christlikeness. "The grace of God that brings salvation has appeared to all men. It teaches us to say 'No' to ungodliness and worldly passions, and to live self-controlled, upright and godly lives in this present age." What a stunning declaration to the life-changing power of God's saving grace. Just as a crossing gate flashes and rings and bars the way when a train is approaching, so the continuing influence of God's saving grace signals "Do Not Cross" to old habits of sinful disobedience.

When the apostle Paul says, "The grace of God that brings salvation has appeared to all men," I take him to mean that it appears to all men *in the same way*. It teaches *all it touches* to live a godly life—not some select group of superdevout Christians, not just monks or clergy. It's not optional to salvation, it's standard equipment. It's part of the grace that brings *salvation*. Other things may be called grace, but they're not *saving* grace. That's why I call it a *glad* obedience. We learn to pray with David,

> I desire to do your will, O my God;
> your law is within my heart. (Psalm 40:8)

We say with Paul, "We make it our goal to please Him" (2 Corinthians 5:9).

Does this mean that Christians *never* feel resistant to God or never want things our way or never feel a desire to please our flesh? It's probably most people's experience that we feel embarrassing amounts of resistance and that our obedience is a halting, sputtering devotion at times. By a glad obedience I mean that the *desire for holiness* is planted in our hearts through faith in Christ. "No one who is born of God will continue to sin, because God's seed remains in him; he cannot go on sinning, because he has been born of God" (1 John 3:9). This seed is God's gift of holiness. It asserts itself against our naturally disobedient and self-centered tendencies so that we wrestle against the evil behavior we used to relish. God's grace lays siege against those sins fortified by habitual practice. Conviction strikes and intensifies. A healthy fear of God and a growing love of God bang away at the habit. The Word of God teaches us the value of repentance and prayer and brotherly accountability, all of which are part of God's continuing grace to free us from habitual sins.

We find an analogy to the steady force of God's grace in the autumn leaves. What makes them cling so tightly throughout the summer, in spite of all the storms that blow through, and then let go on a still autumn day and fall like colored snowflakes? The answer is that underneath the base of the stem, a new bud is forming, pushing, nudging, and eventually unhinging the old leaf. We do not see the evidence of this until six months later when it swells and bursts forth as a new leaf, but it's there nonetheless. In the same way God has put into our heart a new life principle. It's a love for righteousness, and as it grows it nudges old habits till they drop. Over many years we can see this governing principle in the changed life it produces. Or we will not see it and rightly call into question the reality of our repentance and question whether we are under the grace of God.[6]

Does this mean that Christians never sin at all? What about those times when I feel cold toward God and I lose a desire to please Him? Do I lose my standing with God? Sin always costs us something. We are deceived if we think it doesn't. Both Scripture and life experience teach us that love can grow cold and that losing our first love is both possible and costly (Revelation 2:4-5). But one way the Bible answers these questions may be better illustrated than analyzed.

SHEEP STUMBLE BUT SWINE WALLOW

Sheep and swine can both end up in the mire. Yet the essential difference in their two natures is quite visible from the reaction each has to its fallen condition. While sheep do stray and stumble into the mire, they quickly loathe the situation and struggle to get free. They may be dirty, but they desire to be clean. They may be stuck, but they bleat for their shepherd to come and save them out of the muck. But swine, in keeping with their nature, wallow in the muck, content to stay there all day.

When professing Christians behave badly, we are confused by the inconsistency. No matter what one's theology might say about assurance of salvation, where unbelief, disobedience, and sinful habits persist, there is an ever shrinking inner witness of belonging to Christ. Those observing this persistent lack of an obedient heart will also lose confidence. A person who *consistently* says one thing while acting out another is called a hypocrite. Such a person is a liar. "The man who says, 'I know Him,' but does not do what He commands is a liar, and the truth is not in him" (1 John 2:4). Hypocrites are under the wrath of God, no matter how much assurance of grace they claim (Matthew 7:22, 24:51).

But authentic Christians can and do fall under temptation and into the mire of sin. Their actions are often inconsistent with the way of righteousness. It's more a sign of immaturity or weakness, not hypocrisy. The apostle Paul prepares us for this: "Brothers, if someone is caught in a sin, you who are spiritual should restore him gently" (Galatians 6:1).

Contrast this with 1 John 3:6: "No one who lives in [Christ] keeps on sinning." One forewarns us that a brother will be "caught in a sin," the other that true brothers don't continue sinning as before. How do we reconcile these two? I believe the answer goes back to understanding our nature. Do we have a sheep nature or a pig nature? If we have a pig nature, like a pig we will not only fall into the mire but we will scramble for it; we will hunker down into it and roll our backs in it. We will live in sin, defend our sin, and surround ourselves with others in sin.

Every authentic Christian is given a new nature by the regenerating power of God's Spirit (Ezekiel 36:26-27, 1 Peter 1:3). It's the nature of a sheep before a shepherd. We may fall into the mire because we temporarily refuse to follow the shepherd. But once in the mire, we bleat for help and desire to get out. We willingly receive the restoration offered by mature Christians who come to advise us how to overcome our sin through godly sorrow, accountability to others, and growing deeper in the grace of God. This is one way we are "proved genuine" (1 Peter 1:7) and "make [our] calling and election sure" (2 Peter 1:10). Sheep stumble, but swine wallow. What we are may be difficult to discern when we are covered in mud. But our reaction to it, over a period of time, will tell us if we are a part of God's flock or the devil herd.

A JOYFUL ASSURANCE

This brings us to the third part of Jeremiah's description of God's continuing work of grace—a joyful and unshakable assurance of God's full acceptance of us.

"I will be their God,
and they will be my people." (Jeremiah 31:33)

This ultimately is the unshakable ground of our gladness of heart. When the foundation for our everlasting peace with God was laid, the foundation of our everlasting joy in God was laid as well. They share the same foundation. Notice the linkage in Romans 5:1-2: "We have peace with God through our Lord Jesus Christ, through whom we have gained access by faith into this grace in which we now stand. And we rejoice in the hope of the glory of God." Where *peace with God* is established, *pleasure in God* erupts. This pleasure is in knowing that God accepts us and always will.

Our abiding faith in Christ so pleases God that His wrath is removed and His happiness in us knows no limit. What firmer foundation could there be for our own gladness than to know that God delights in us who put our faith in Christ? Our assurance that He is pleased with us, delighted with us, rejoices over us, is unrestrainable in loving us, and won't be robbed of the joy of welcoming us into His presence is all the assurance we need to rejoice in Him daily and be confident that our new relationship with Him is rooted in an everlasting covenant. We are the Lord's treasured possession, the sheep of His pasture. This assurance is part of the gift of God's grace.

God has left us a clear testimony that He delights in His people. Isaiah 62:4 says,

No longer will they call you Deserted,
    or name your land Desolate.
But you will be called Hephzibah [my delight],
    and your land Beulah [married];
for the LORD will take delight in you,
    and your land will be married.

God's delight in His people caused Him to plan and pursue us as a man pursues the love of his life. I remember how I plotted and arranged to marry my wife, Kristen. There were

talking points to be broached ever so delicately. Feelings had
to be confirmed and solidified. There were fears to allay and
expectations to be understood. There was a formal proposal to
be made, and that had its own planning and preparation to it—
all very enjoyable. There was shopping to be done—for not
just any diamond ring but the right one. How can I find out
what she likes? How can I earn the money to buy it? More planning and plotting. Then schedules needed to be considered,
and arrangements for our life together after the wedding needed
to be thought through. With ring in hand, further plots had to
be hatched, surprises had to be set up. All of this joy was in
just the anticipation of our union.

Then there is the joy of making the actual proposal. At the
solemn moment I breathed deeply and asked Kristen to marry
me. With joy I slid the ring on her finger. This joy kept building as the wedding was planned over the following months. The
rehearsal heightened the joy because it signaled the nearness of
the consummation. Then of course there is the consummation
itself, formally as she stepped down the long aisle in all her radi-
ance and splendor and we pledged to live together faithfully, as
long as we both shall live. Then of course there is the intimate
and intense joy of consummated love as two become one flesh.
Eighteen years later, how does one find words to explain the joy
of companionship through all the disappointments, setbacks,
and hardships of life?

God's joy over us is exactly like this, only purer and deeper.
How can we be so sure? Because Isaiah 62:5 says,

As a bridegroom rejoices over his bride,
 so will God rejoice over you.

He enjoys the wooing of our heart's affection away from sin and
self to Himself. He delights to make a vow to us and delights in
our vow to be faithful to Him all our days. As His bride we are
united with Him through the Spirit He gives us.

Even the Cross, with its unspeakable suffering and humili-
ating shame, was motivated by the *joy* Christ anticipated in

winning us to God. "Let us fix our eyes on Jesus, the author and perfecter of our faith, who for the joy set before Him endured the cross, scorning its shame" (Hebrews 12:2). The joy He saw was the delight of having us united to Him as a bride. "Christ loved the church and gave himself up for her to make her holy, . . . to present her to himself as a radiant church" (Ephesians 5:25-27). Because we are His beloved people, He says, "I will rejoice in doing them good . . . with all my heart and soul" (Jeremiah 32:41). This union has taken place through our faith, and as long as we remain faithful we can rest assured of our full acceptance by Him.

> If we endure,
> we will also reign with Him. (2 Timothy 2:12)

HARDSHIP IS NO LASTING IMPEDIMENT TO A GLAD HEART

There are times when events and circumstances make us feel like God has rejected us. On these occasions our tears are our food night and day. We question if God has turned His back on us or forgotten us. We can feel such numbing pain and loss at certain times that living seems a terrible burden. We openly wonder how we can go on. How do we reconcile this reality with the unshakable gladness of heart that is ours in the grace of God?

In this life, tears and joy are only incompatible if we fail to remember that our joy is *in God* and not tethered to any current circumstances in this temporal life.

> I delight greatly *in the* LORD;
> my soul rejoices *in my God.*
> For He has clothed me with garments of salvation
> and arrayed me in a robe of righteousness. (Isaiah 61:10)

Jesus agonized on the cross for the joy of something beyond the cross.

√ So with us, our emotions are linked to our present circumstances and life experiences, but peace and joy are deeper than emotions. Emotions rise and fall as we experience on a rotating basis poverty and plenty, good health and sickness, a few good breaks and then a string of "bad luck." Into every person's life story are written unexpected tragedy and suffering and the certainty of sickness and death. This present life offers only fleeting pleasures and seasons of good times. The gladness of heart we are talking about is deeper and higher than this world. It's nothing less than an abiding, trusting confidence in God's goodness in spite of present experiences; and it's not uncommon for the deepest peace and our most unspeakable joy in God to come in the midst of tremendous personal trauma. We experience joy as a ballast keeping our ship afloat throughout the raging storms of life, not as sunshine.

Horatio Spafford (1828-1888) was a prosperous lawyer in Chicago in the years following the Civil War. He invested his money in shoreline property on Lake Michigan and was able to give generously to the work of Christian ministry, using his buildings to help reach the urban poor and to contribute to the global ministries of his personal friends, the famous evangelist D. L. Moody and the well-known hymn writer, Philip Bliss. Spafford had a wife and five children—four daughters and a son. Then a series of tragedies hit Spafford that would break the faith of anyone not anchored in the true grace of the gospel.

First their young son died of pneumonia. As Spafford and his wife struggled in their grief, their friends urged them to take a vacation to England and join Moody in his campaigns there. Spafford resisted because he was at that time renovating some buildings in Chicago to help the YMCA outreach. Then in 1871, just four months after the death of their son, the Great Chicago Fire hit, burning two thousand acres of property, including all of Spafford's. His friends again urged him to get away and rest. Little could be done about the loss. He arranged passage to London for his family and himself, except that two days before departure he was forced to appear before officials who were trying to sort out ownership claims. Spafford sent his family ahead and planned to follow on the next boat.

A few days into the crossing, the ship collided with another in a fog bank. It sank in twelve minutes. The initial reports were very hopeful; there were many survivors. Then Spafford received a telegram from his wife: "Come quickly, I alone survive. Your beloved wife."

All four of his young daughters were gone. As he steamed for London he asked the captain to notify him when the ship reached the point where his daughters went down. There he wept and poured out his heart to God. As he watched the sea billows roll he thought of God, His sovereignty, His mercy, and all His promises. Then he wrote down his thoughts and, later, his friend Philip Bliss put them to music. The result has become one of the church's greatest hymns of praise, "It Is Well with My Soul."

When peace like a river attendeth my way,
    When sorrows like sea billows roll—
Whatever my lot, thou hast taught me to say,
    It is well, it is well, with my soul.

Tho' Satan should buffet, tho trials should come,
    Let this blest assurance control,
that Christ hath regarded my helpless estate
    And hath shed His own blood for my soul.

My sin—O the bliss of this glorious tho't—
    My sin, not in part, but the whole,
Is nailed to the cross, and I bear it no more:
    Praise the Lord, praise the Lord, O my soul!

And Lord, haste the day when my faith shall be sight,
    The clouds be rolled back as a scroll:
The trump shall resound and the Lord shall descend,
    "Even so"—it is well with my soul.

Spafford's gladness makes room for much weeping. But it will not be overcome. Our gladness is in God, and ultimately, in God alone. This gladness is inaccessible to the darkest powers of this corrupt world. No one can take away our joy unless he can figure a way to take God away from our hearts. In the history of God's saving grace, no example of this has yet been found. Tragedy cannot. Persecution cannot. Poverty cannot. As Romans 8:35-39 says:

> Who shall separate us from the love of Christ? Shall trouble or hardship or persecution or famine or nakedness or danger or sword? . . . No, in all these things we are more than conquerors through Him who loved us. For I am convinced that neither death nor life, neither angels nor demons, neither the present nor the future, nor any powers, neither height nor depth, nor anything else in all creation, will be able to separate us from the love of God that is in Christ Jesus our Lord.

THE GLORY OF THE ORDINARY CHRISTIAN
UNDER THE INFLUENCE

Horatio Spafford was an extraordinary Christian in many ways, a great inspiration to our faith. But I think it better to close this chapter with the most average Christian I know. After all, God promised continuing grace to all His people, "from the least of them to the greatest" (Jeremiah 31:34). Average Christians, with more mundane life experiences, undergo the same influence of God's grace. And there is glory here too.

Gene is the most ordinary man I've ever met. He's average in height and appearance, in intelligence and skills. He loves pizza and sports. Nothing about Gene is going to grab your attention. He's never going to write a book or sing or run for office or lead events. Yet Gene is a hero to me because, by his quiet and God-honoring life, he has demonstrated the power of living under the influence of God's grace.

Though Gene's stepfather has been dead for some years, Gene's memories of him are painful and stir up bitterness inside him. Gene's reluctant to speak about his stepfather, and he acknowledges the struggle to forgive.

While Gene is reluctant to speak of his own woundedness, he's open about his waywardness. In his twenties Gene was drinking and drugging himself into oblivion. Several times he was homeless, and as he says, "properly so." One day Gene woke up from a drunken stupor to realize that he drank a can of beer that had been used as an ashtray. Gene knew he was in trouble. He went to detox repeatedly. But it was only temporary help he sought. Once he was sober for a whole year, then took one drink and within a week was getting plastered every night. He was alienated from his family, from society, from himself, from God. Then Gene gave his life to Christ.

What happened as a result? Did he become a great leader, write a great hymn, start a famous ministry, or lobby for great social justice? No, but he was enabled to maintain his sobriety. A year later he gave up smoking. For several years he worked steadily as a taxi driver and then started painting houses. He went to church every Sunday, attended various Bible studies, and began to serve the people there as needed.

A few years later he fell in love with a woman in my church and for three years he gently and persistently pursued her. I took them through premarital counseling and conducted their wedding. In the meantime, Gene went to school for computer-assisted design (CAD). When he finished he couldn't find work. I suggested he contact an architect and offer to work for free just to put something on his résumé. His brother-in-law suggested the same thing and even told him where he might apply. He did and it worked. Soon he had a full-time but temporary job. No more taxi driving for Gene. After two years of marriage they bought their first house. This spring, at forty, Gene and his wife had their first baby.

During these years, Gene has served in his church and supported several missions, including our inner-city counseling center. Recently Gene handed me his very first business card. It had his name on it and the name of the company he is now working for as a permanent employee. All this change happened slowly but steadily over a fifteen-year period.

First Thessalonians 4:11-12 says, "Make it your ambition to lead a quiet life, to mind your own business and to work with your hands, just as we told you, so that your daily life may win the respect of outsiders and so that you will not be dependent on anybody." This is Gene's testimony. It's a good testimony and full of glory in its own way. Most of us are average and ordinary. Yet we too will greatly glorify God's mercy in our lives if, like Gene, we learn to live under the ongoing influence of God's grace. In one matter after another, let us look to God with a thankful heart, follow His ways, and rest in the assurance of His love. This is our inheritance as recipients of the gift of God's forgiveness.

<hr />

The Journey from Guilt to Gladness

Under the influence of God's continuing grace, God slowly yet persistently changes our speech, our personal habits, our demeanor, our priorities in life, and our decisions. He teaches us how to live, how to love, and how to serve. Learning to live under the influence of God's grace is the next step from guilt to gladness.

Chapter Nine

Forgiveness Shared

PUSHING PAST GRUDGES

*Of him that hopes to be forgiven, it is indespensibly required
that he forgive. On this great duty eternity is to be suspended.*
—SAMUEL JOHNSON, *THE RAMBLER*

☙

*If you do not forgive men their sins,
your Father will not forgive your sins.*
—MATTHEW 6:15

As a student at Bethel College, I remember the late Dr. Carl
Lundquist saying, "You never really find out what's inside
a man until he's bumped and you see what spills out." He was
illustrating the link between forgiveness received and forgiveness extended—a link so strong that the one confirms the presence of the other. God in His providence insures that we all get
plenty of chances to show what's inside us. We'll suffer these
bumps with either increasing bitterness or as our finest moments
when the grace of God unmistakably and radiantly spills forth.
Therefore, learning to push past grudges is crucial to growing
winsome and healthy as a Christian and finally obtaining the
full measure of grace that brings eternal life.[1]

THE NECESSITY OF FORGIVING
THOSE WHO HURT YOU

If we have experienced God's forgiveness, we are under a moral
imperative to forgive others. The apostle Paul called it "the

obedience that comes from faith" (Romans 1:5). This means we obey God, not in order to win His favor and earn His mercy, but out of our growing confidence in Him as our God. Daniel Fuller's illustration is worth remembering. He said that when I obey my doctor's orders I am expressing faith in my doctor. If I don't, my doctor will say, "Find a doctor you *trust*," meaning one you'll *obey*.[2] One of the clearest orders given by the Great Physician of our souls is that we *must* forgive those we hold grudges against: "Forgive your brother from your heart," He said (Matthew 18:35).

From the earliest days, those who received grace and mercy from the Lord were compelled to extend it toward those who hurt them. God delivered Israel from bondage and established a relationship based on faith, saying, "I will walk among you and be your God, and you will be my people" (Leviticus 26:12). As their Sovereign Lord, God commanded them,

> "Do not hate your brother in your heart. Rebuke your neighbor frankly so you will not share in his guilt.
>
> Do not seek revenge or bear a grudge against one of your people, but love your neighbor as yourself. I am the LORD." (Leviticus 19:17-18)

Notice that the command to forgive does not mean denying the reality of someone's evil or rationalizing the wrong into a justifiable right (that's what the wrongdoer does). There's a place to call sin sinful and wrongdoing wrong. Silence can be a form of passive agreement with what's going on. "Rebuke your neighbor frankly so you will not share in his guilt," we are told. But that done, God commands us to stay clear of hatred, thoughts of revenge, and the harboring of grudges. What's more, He commands us to love the unlovely people in our lives! The basis of this command is our faith in God as the watchman of our soul's health and happiness. "I am your God."

When God became a man and lived among us, He reaffirmed the necessity of getting past grudges. Jesus prohibits us from seeking revenge or even from pondering spiteful thoughts.

We are directed to consider how to *help* those who hurt us. "You have heard that it was said, 'Love your neighbor and hate your enemy.' But I tell you: Love your enemies and pray for those who persecute you, that you may be sons of your Father in heaven" (Matthew 5:43-45). What kind of people can love like this? Only children of the heavenly Father. The children of heaven bleed grace when cut by others, and they receive a transfusion of grace in the process!

Anyone can live out the puny ethical creed "You scratch my back and I'll scratch yours." The children of God have a higher calling. "If you love those who love you, what credit is that to you? Even 'sinners' love those who love them" (Luke 6:32). When we return love for hatred, and prayer for a curse, eyebrows are raised. People see that God is in us because God's grace is spilling forth from us.

We all know how hard forgiving someone from the heart can be. It ought not surprise us that Jesus follows His command to forgive others with an instruction on how to pray. *Prayer is faith articulating its glad dependence on God's provision.* In what's commonly called the "Our Father" or the Lord's Prayer, Jesus teaches us to pray in such a way that we connect our strong desire to be forgiven to our weak desire to forgive others. We are to pray,

> "Our Father in heaven,
> hallowed be your name. . . .
> Forgive us our debts [sins],
> > as we also have forgiven our debtors [those who've sinned against us]. . . .
>
> > For if you forgive men when they sin against you, your heavenly Father will also forgive you. But if you do not forgive men their sins, your Father will not forgive your sins." (Matthew 6:9,12,14-15)

The authenticity and beauty of my friend Stephen's conversion are entirely understood by the prayer, "Forgive us our debts, *as* we forgive our debtors." I only knew Stephen for the last two years of his life. Stephen was an Irish cussing cowboy wannabe. Born and raised on the streets of Boston, he moved to Texas for many years. There he ran guns, drank heavily, and fought with anybody he could bait by his small size—a dangerous lifestyle for a hemophiliac. In the mid-eighties he contracted the AIDS virus through tainted blood. Back in Boston, his brother, an elder in my church, prayed and waited.

One day Stephen learned that the boyfriend of a baby-sitter hired to watch his infant daughter was annoyed by the baby's crying. He beat the child and threw her out in the back yard, where she was bitten by fire ants. She died a horrible death and her killer was arrested and sent to prison. It was the hardest blow of Stephen's life, and he returned to Boston a broken yet seething man. In spite of many invitations, he refused to come to church. Every time I went over to the house, he scurried upstairs and out of sight.

A few months later his brother, Tom, got arrested for participating in a nonviolent sit-in at an abortion clinic. He went there, he said, as an act of repentance for the three abortions he was personally responsible for years earlier. In the pain over the murder of his own child, Stephen wanted to protest the killing of innocent children and so attended and got arrested at a subsequent sit-in in West Hartford, Connecticut.

Along with about three hundred other men and women, he was held in a state prison for almost a week before being released. Every day the men gathered for prayer, and Stephen heard many testimonies and heartfelt prayers. About midweek, while in a circle of praying men, he started to weep. Then he prayed. "God, I pray that You would *forgive* the man who murdered my daughter . . . forgive him . . . and please forgive me, too, for all I've done."

Stephen clearly wanted peace with God. But he realized that to have it, he must forgive his enemy. He prayed just as Christ taught us all to pray: "Forgive us our sins, *as* we forgive those who've sinned against us."

Stephen came out of that prison radically changed. He was

radically tenderized. He showed great concern for others, especially the weak and the sick. He joked and laughed and enjoyed visiting with people. He came alive, even while he was dying. He visited Texas to set some things right with his ex-wife, then returned to Boston to live out his last days. His willingness to forgive the man he hated most in this world caused him to experience his own heartfelt forgiveness from God. His last months were spent in a hospice, mostly with homosexuals dying of AIDS. While he could, he shuffled around visiting each one, telling a joke, cursing the sickness, telling them how he had received God's mercy, and praying with them. He died in great pain and in great peace.

There are many people who have blocked the flow of mercy in their own lives with huge grudges. Stephen knew somehow that his own ability to receive mercy was dependent on letting go of his grudges — no matter how justified they felt. A wise puritan once said, "He that demands mercy and shows none, ruins the bridge over which he himself is to pass."[3] So Stephen forgave his worst enemy and in so doing received mercy from God.

JESUS, OUR EXAMPLE

Showing mercy to our adversaries is something Jesus not only taught but demonstrated. Peter said He is our "example" of how to push past grudges (1 Peter 2:21). Though He was the incarnate love of God, full of grace and truth, and sinned against no one, yet He was betrayed by a disciple, falsely accused by those He came to serve, abandoned by His friends, humiliated and beaten, and hammered to death. "When they hurled their insults at Him, He did not retaliate; when He suffered, He made no threats. Instead, He entrusted himself to Him who judges justly" (1 Peter 2:23). His pain was fuel for prayer. "Father, forgive them, for they do not know what they are doing" (Luke 23:34). We, too, must pray like this for those who've hurt us, and keep on praying. Persistent grudges must be met with persevering prayer until we obtain the grace to forgive.

In spite of Jesus' example and the testimony of people like Stephen, I've never talked with anyone struggling with the inflammation and hurt caused by another who didn't insist that I appreciate how *hard*, how nearly impossible it was to forgive those he or she was holding a grudge against. "If you only understood how badly they hurt me," the logic goes, "you wouldn't expect me to forgive them."

I have enough of my own raw experiences to realize that this is pain talking. Grudges love to be nursed, not nuked. Given enough time and fertilizer, our grudges will grow so big they will wrap themselves around our very personality and cover us like ivy covers a house. We'll soon think and talk as victims of our hurt rather than as victors over it. Some people would feel disoriented without their grudges. Such people are doomed unless and until they let go of their grudges. They're like people crying out for a life preserver but refusing to let go of the anchor! We have to choose one. "If you do not forgive men their sins, your Father will not forgive your sins" (Matthew 6:15). This cannot be more blunt. Our grip on grudges must be released. Our very life depends on it.

THE RIGHTNESS OF FORGIVING OTHERS

Why can God be so unequivocal about conditioning our forgiveness on the willingness to forgive others?[4] Jesus answered this question with a parable. He tells of a king who was owed millions of dollars by one of his subjects. When a servant couldn't pay his debt, the king ordered the man, his wife, and his children to prison. The man begged for time. He promised to pay back everything. Instead, the king showed how merciful he could be. He tore up his debt and let him go free. What followed in the parable demonstrates the wickedness of someone receiving mercy and yet withholding mercy.

> "When that servant went out, he found one of his fellow servants who owed him a hundred denarii [a few dollars]. He grabbed him and began to choke him. 'Pay back what you owe me!' he demanded.

"His fellow servant fell to his knees and begged him,
'Be patient with me, and I will pay you back.'
"But he refused. Instead, he went off and had the man
thrown into prison until he could pay the debt."
(Matthew 18:28-30)

Here is an example of a man who acts in faith, all right—
bad faith. When the king hears about it, he summons the servant and denounces him. He orders him to prison to pay all his
debts. Then Jesus says to us, "This is how my heavenly Father
will treat each of you unless you forgive your brother from your
heart" (18:35). God will not tolerate His mercy to be treated with
contempt. We would have more sympathy if the story ran that
the servant throttled the other servant for his few dollars because
he had his own huge debt to repay and could expect no grace
from the king. The outrage comes in the exercise of bad faith;
having begged for mercy while having none for others.

That is why I say forgiving others is crucial to finally obtaining the full measure of grace that brings eternal life. Initially,
when someone asks humbly, confesses their need, and praises
God for His forgiveness, we naturally will assume and hope that
genuine saving faith has begun. But time confirms or denies the
saving nature of our initial plea for mercy. If it proves out to be
bad faith by the bad reflection it casts toward others, then it will
be exposed as such. If our faith produces a gracious spirit toward
others, it will be rewarded with everlasting grace.

SAND IN THE EYE

Most of the wounds we bear come from people whose selfish-
ness and pride lead them to say and do insensitive things. Often
they are loved ones. Sometimes they're acting out of their own
unmet needs, past hurts, and quiet rebellion against the lord-
ship of God. They inflict real hurts, but they're not consciously
out to destroy us. Unfortunately we can't say that about everyone. In pushing past grudges, it's helpful to distinguish between
those hurts that come from being offended and those that come

from being violated. One is more of an irritant; the other more of an injury. Of course, we can turn all our irritants into injuries.

On occasion the wind will gust and a speck of grit or sand will blow into our eye, slip in under the lid, and at once irritate us something terrible. Our first urge is to rub our eye furiously. But only a fool acts on that urge. We hold back because we know that rubbing the sand in our eye only makes a bad situation worse. If rubbed, the whole eye will be inflamed and, perhaps, permanently damaged.

Similar urges and possible damage result when others irritate us by what they say or how they act, especially because they do it over and over and over again. We can slough it off once, maybe twice, and think ourselves gracious, but by the third time we are looking for a two-by-four and contemplating how many whacks it will take to correct the problem. They've gotten under our skin and irritated our very souls. Brooding over the behavior of others is like rubbing the sand in our eye. It doesn't take long before that relationship is raw and supersensitive. But the truth is, it was only a speck. It was a small irritant. It need not have caused us any real or lasting harm.

Jesus prepared us for these sand-in-the-eye experiences.

> Peter came to Jesus and asked, "Lord, how many times shall I forgive my brother when he sins against me? Up to seven times?"
>
> Jesus answered, "I tell you, not seven times, but seventy-seven times." (Matthew 18:21-22)

We never get off the hook of mercy shared! As children of God and vessels of His grace, we are not allowed to count. We are not allowed to say, "That's the last straw." If it *is* the last straw, you're counting! What are we to do then?

We are to love. What tears do for our eyes, love does for our souls. Love washes away irritants before they harm us. Forgiveness is God's love expressing its desire to push past grudges. Love forgives. Love is patient and forbearing. Since God loves us like this, we are to love others the same way. "I urge you to live

a life worthy of the calling you have received. Be completely humble and gentle; be patient, bearing with one another in love" (Ephesians 4:1-2). God's love also expresses itself as forgetfulness. "[Love] is not easily angered, it keeps no record of wrongs" (1 Corinthians 13:5). Love, in its various forms of self-expression (patience, forbearance, forgiveness, forgetfulness), like tears in the eyes, washes away the sting of harsh words, thoughtless words, ill-timed words. Love purges out slights, a false witness against us, a betrayed confidence, an ill temper, and hundreds of other irritations that gust up into our hearts.

The person who wants to walk in God's love learns to love others. We learn to love the unlovely, and continue to do so for as long as we would like God to love us. Gary Thomas, the Christian commentator for *World* magazine, recently wrote, "Mature Christians have a double standard. They are hard on themselves when it comes to sin, but gracious and gentle toward others."[5]

Most of the strained relationships we have are due to sand in the eye that is rubbed raw. We've tried changing the person, attacking the person, giving the person the cold shoulder, or running from the person. But the hook holds. The will of God is loving the person, forgiving the person from the heart, and forbearing with the person. So we are commanded,

> Bear with each other and forgive whatever grievances you may have against one another. Forgive as the Lord forgave you. And over all these virtues put on love, which binds them all together in perfect unity. (Colossians 3:13-14)

I saw a vivid picture of this once when visiting a family who had a large German shepherd and a small child. While we were talking, the toddler toddled in and jumped on the big dog while it lay quietly on the floor. This dog, which can be a fierce watchdog, and certainly checked me out when I came to the door, was startled and disturbed. He felt the blow. But he looked up, saw who it was, and laid its head back down. I sat there amazed watching the youngster roll around on the dog, pull its hair, playfully push and shove and make a nuisance of himself to the dog. The dog endured it all. He never snapped or growled, in spite of getting stepped on and yanked about pretty well. The dog's behavior said, "It's just that immature little tyke. He's no threat, just an annoyance, and I can take it." The gift of God includes the capacity to love like that, bearing with the immature, the annoying, and the inconsiderate.

FALLING PREY TO THE WICKED

Some of us have fallen prey to genuinely wicked people. We are no longer talking about sand in the eye but fangs in the flesh. Psalm 52:7 identifies the nature of a wicked man.

> Here now is the man
>   who did not make God his stronghold
> but trusted in his great wealth
>   and grew strong by destroying others!

The wicked person grows strong by destroying others. Such people deceive, seduce, exploit, inflict pain—and enjoy every step in the process. They have brutalized and betrayed others and laughed about it. They see every relationship as a win-lose competition. Everyone is to be conquered, and anyone who gets the best of them is the target of revenge. They wear suits and smile as often as they hang on corners and dress like thugs. They are rich and poor, male and female.

Make no mistake about whether some people are truly wicked. When a mother sticks her child's hand in boiling water for childish behavior, that's wicked and the wound goes far deeper than the burned flesh. That happened in my city. I ached with the young woman in our counseling center who told me that when she was fourteen, her mother's boyfriend came to her one afternoon and raped her. When she told her mother about it that night, *she* was kicked out of her own house, not the boyfriend. Her mother considered her daughter as competition.

Irina Ratushinskaya spent *seven* years as a prisoner in a gulag for writing poetry about human rights and about the Lord who gave them. After she was reunited with her husband, they learned that officials were going to return and arrest her husband. By God's grace they were able to get out and write about the experience.[6] There is no shortage of evil plots, torture, and death being played out in various parts of the world at any one time. History is a catalog of human wickedness, rising and falling and rising again.

David fell prey to a wicked man by the name of Doeg. At the time David was falsely accused of betraying King Saul and had to flee for his life (1 Samuel 19:1). Even though David was innocent of all wrongdoing (20:1), he was forced to live in caves and find food as best he could to survive. He went to the house of Ahimelech, a faithful priest in the city of Nob, who gave him food. "Now one of Saul's servants was there that day, detained before the LORD; he was Doeg the Edomite" (21:7). Later on, Doeg reported to Saul what the priest had done for David. "Ahimelech inquired of the LORD for him; he also gave him provisions" (22:10). Doeg knew that his report endangered the priest, but he wanted to ingratiate himself with Saul. He wanted to *grow stronger by destroying others.*

Ahimelech and his entire family were summoned. The other priests in Nob who failed to report the incident were also summoned and accused of treason. Saul ordered them *all* killed. Saul's soldiers refused to kill the priests because they were innocent and "priests of the LORD" (22:17). So Saul said to Doeg, "You turn and strike down the priests" (22:18). Doeg did, and "that day he killed eighty-five men who wore the linen ephod. He also put to the sword Nob, the town of the priests, with its men and women, its children and infants" (22:18-19). Doeg slaughtered the entire village to be strong in the eyes of Saul. David broke when he learned of it. He felt partly responsible for it. He wrote Psalm 52 out of the anguish inflicted by the wicked. Perhaps you recognize a description of your own Doeg in his words:

> Why do you boast of evil, you mighty man?
>> Why do you boast all day long,
>>> you who are a disgrace in the eyes of God?

Your tongue plots destruction;
    it is like a sharpened razor,
    you who practice deceit.
You love evil rather than good,
    falsehood rather than speaking the truth. (verses 1-3)

The suffering such people cause is beyond measure, and their punishment is well deserved. But David plots no revenge. He makes room for the judgment of the Lord to deal with his Doeg, as we must ours.

Surely God will bring you down to everlasting ruin:
    He will snatch you up and tear you from your tent;
    He will uproot you from the land of the living. (verse 5)

It's not wrong to draw comfort from the vindicating right-eousness of God. God reassures us that He sees the wicked things men do and will avenge the pain they cause. "Do not take revenge, my friends," wrote the apostle Paul, "but leave room for God's wrath, for it is written: 'It is mine to avenge; I will repay'" (Romans 12:19). The promise of God's vindicating wrath frees us from the entangling impulse of acting as a judge and executioner. We may leave it to God and comfort ourselves with Psalm 37:5-9:

Commit your way to the LORD;
    trust in Him and He will do this:
He will make your righteousness shine like the dawn,
    the justice of your cause like the noonday sun.

Be still before the LORD and wait patiently for Him;
    do not fret when men succeed in their ways,
    when they carry out their wicked schemes.

Refrain from anger and turn from wrath;
    do not fret—it leads only to evil.
For evil men will be cut off,
    but those who hope in the LORD will inherit the land.

Holding on to grudges and contemplating revenge is an expression of no confidence in God acting righteously. We need to trust God for our vindication and go on in love.

HOW DO WE PUSH PAST OUR GRUDGES?

Romans 12:21 says, "Do not be overcome by evil, but overcome evil with good." How do we overcome evil with good? We overcome evil by getting an *overwhelming* vision of the goodness of God. His goodness empowers us to forgive those who've hurt us deeply. Therefore we need to see God's goodness and learn to trust in it. We do that in three ways.

Trusting God's Commands

Trusting that God's commands are good gives us the power to forgive. Psalm 119:39-40 says,

> Your laws are good.
> How I long for your precepts!
> Preserve my life in your righteousness.

When we don't feel like doing what we know is God's will, our love for Him and our deeper trust in the goodness of His word will overcome our reluctance. This is especially true in dealing with the natural resistance we feel to forgiving others.

Corrie ten Boom's struggle to forgive is well known in Christian circles, but it's worth repeating since it shows the importance of trusting in God's word. During World War II Corrie and her family rescued Jews from slaughter by hiding them in their house. They were betrayed, caught, and sent to Ravensbruck concentration camp. More than 96,000 women died there, one of whom was her beloved sister, Betsy. Corrie, prisoner 366730, survived. A few years later, in 1947, Corrie gave a speech at a church in Munich, after which a heavyset man approached her. Corrie recognized him as one of the most brutal guards in her camp. She froze in pain and anguish. The man said to her, "Since that time, I have become a Christian. I know that God has forgiven me for the cruel things I did there, but I would like to hear it from your lips as well. Fraulein—will you forgive me?" Corrie wrestled with what she said was the most difficult thing she ever did. She wrote,

> I had to do it—I knew that. The message that God forgives has a prior condition: that we forgive those who have injured us. "Jesus, help me!" I prayed silently. "I can lift my hand. I can do that much. You supply the feeling."
>
> And so woodenly, mechanically, I thrust my hand into the one stretched out to me. And as I did, an incredible thing took place. The current started in my shoulder, raced down my arm, sprang into our joined hands. And then this healing warmth seemed to flood my whole being, bringing tears to my eyes.
>
> "I forgive you, brother!" I cried. "With all my heart!"
>
> For a long moment we grasped each other's hands, the former guard and the former prisoner. I had never known God's love so intensely as I did then.[7]

I like Corrie's honesty; her account rings true. God must supply the grace to forgive. But one way He does that is through our trust in the goodness of His commands. In the battle we face over our conflicting emotions, trusting in the goodness of God's word, and so obeying Him, will break the logjam and bring us the mercy of God we so desperately need to share.

Trusting God's Sovereignty
Trusting in God's sovereignty also gives us the power to forgive. To trust that God is sovereign is to trust that God is not up in heaven ringing His hands, saying, "Things have gotten out of control! What am I to do!" To trust in God's sovereignty means to trust that He is in control and working for our good in all things, even through evil. Because God is sovereign, Proverbs 16:4 can say,

> The LORD works out everything for His own ends—
> even the wicked for a day of disaster.

That is why the Bible says He *caused* His own Son to suffer (Isaiah 53:10), because it was Him working out everything for His own ends, even though His death was actually caused by wicked men (and the provocation of Satan). Men do wicked things and are accountable for it. God's sovereignty means that He forces even wicked behavior to serve His ultimate good.

God's sovereignty is declared in Romans 8:28 as a comfort to wounded believers. "We know that in *all* things God works for the *good* of those who love Him, who have been called according to His purpose". God isn't working for everyone's benefit. He's working toward the defeat and punishment of the wicked. But for those who have the call of God on their life, God assures us that He uses even our bad experiences for a good purpose.

Joseph trusted in God's sovereignty. He was the favorite son of the patriarch Jacob, the second youngest of twelve brothers. At one point Jacob made a richly ornamented robe for Joseph. "When his brothers saw that their father loved [Joseph] more than any of them, they hated him and could not speak a kind word to him" (Genesis 37:4). Favoritism, as plenty of people can testify, is a deeply painful sin and sows deep resentment in those not favored.

Joseph kindled his brothers' bitterness even more by boasting over a dream God gave him. He dreamed that one day he would actually rule his older brothers. He saw them bowing down to him, and he *told them so* (37:5-7). Such a direct challenge to the pecking order created an insatiable desire to give Joseph his comeuppance.

One day they got Joseph alone and plotted to kill him. "'Here comes that dreamer!' they said to each other. 'Come now, let's kill him and throw him into one of these cisterns and say that a ferocious animal devoured him. Then we'll see what comes of his dreams'" (37:19-20). At the last minute his brother Judah rescued him from murder by suggesting they sell him into slavery to a group traveling to Egypt. This had the benefit of sparing them from actual bloodguilt. They could still deceive their father into thinking Joseph was dead, and line their pockets as well. They sold Joseph into slavery, took his fine coat, smeared it in goat's blood, and presented it to their father feigning deep concern: "'We found this.' . . . [Jacob] recognized it and said, 'It is my son's robe! Some ferocious animal has devoured him. Joseph has surely been torn to pieces'" (Genesis 37:32-33). Jacob tore his clothes in grief while his sons rejoiced secretly.

In Egypt, Joseph suffered the humiliation of slavery for many years. Then things got worse. He was falsely accused of sexual harassment and attempted rape (39:1-20). Though innocent, he languished in prison for many more years.

Stop and consider how angry you would be if you suffered such treatment for so many years. How angry would you be at God? If I didn't know God's sovereignty and His promise to be working for my good in all things, I would accuse Him of either impotence (not able to stop evil) or child abuse ("You have treated me badly because You could have stopped this but didn't").

Joseph suffered betrayal by his own family. He was exploited as a worker, falsely accused by one he faithfully served, and subjected to barbaric conditions in prison. Through it all he trusted in his sovereign God and worshiped Him rather than contemplating revenge. "While Joseph was there in the prison, the LORD was with him" (39:20-21).

At one point, with God's help, he rightly interpreted the dreams of two fellow prisoners. Both had been employed by Pharaoh, one as a cupbearer and the other as a baker (40:1-23). The cupbearer's dream, Joseph said, promised deliverance and restoration. The thankful prisoner promised to help secure Joseph's release if the interpretation proved true. It did. Pharaoh "restored the chief cupbearer to his position, so that he once again put the cup into Pharaoh's hand. . . . The chief cupbearer, however, did not remember Joseph; he forgot him" (40:21,23). It doesn't take much to imagine how this final betrayal would hurt and embitter the soul. In today's society, he could go on a rampage, plunder, kill, and drown his pain in drugs and swill, and many therapists and judges would blame it on his woundedness and excuse his waywardness. Instead, Joseph continued to trust in God's sovereignty. He was living out God's will for his life for a purpose he still could not see, but didn't need to see. One day Pharaoh had a dream about cows. The cupbearer remembered Joseph, and he was summoned before Pharaoh to listen to and interpret Pharaoh's dream. Joseph told him:

> God has revealed to Pharaoh what He is about to do. The seven good cows are seven years . . . [and] the seven lean, ugly cows that came up afterward are seven years. . . . They are seven years of famine. (Genesis 41:25-27)

Pharaoh put Joseph in charge over all Egypt to store up food during the seven good years to bring the country through the seven years of famine. When the years of famine came, people from all over came to Egypt to buy food—even Joseph's brothers (42: 1-2). So many years had passed since that awful day when they sold their own brother into slavery that they did not recognize Joseph when they stood before him, and "bowed down to him with their faces to the ground" (42:6), begging to buy food. Joseph recognized them and could have taken out his revenge on the spot.

Instead, Joseph saw the sovereign guidance of God fulfilling the promise given to him in the dream he received in his youth. He saw how God had used his own sin, his boastful arrogance, to spark an even greater and longer-term evil by his brothers. This set in motion all the other injustices that followed, that worked for still a greater good (saving his family). Joseph saw that God's good purposes not only used evil, but *required* evil. Joseph said,

> Do not be distressed and do not be angry with yourselves for selling me here, because it was to save lives that God sent me ahead of you. . . . God sent me ahead of you to preserve for you a remnant on earth and to save your lives by a great deliverance. (45:5-7)

This is the power of knowing God's sovereignty. The brothers *sold* him, but God *sent* him!

Joseph illustrates how trusting in God's sovereignty can give someone the power to forgive. When Joseph's father died, the brothers were terrified and said, "What if Joseph holds a grudge against us and pays us back for all the wrongs we did to him?" Instead of asking forgiveness, they lied again (some people just never change).

> They sent word to Joseph, saying, "Your father left these instructions before he died: 'This is what you are to say to Joseph: I ask you to forgive your brothers the sins and the wrongs they committed in treating you so badly.' Now please forgive the sins of the servants of the God of your father." (50:16-17)

Joseph's response shows the power of trusting God's sovereignty.

> When their message came to him, Joseph wept. . . . Joseph said to them, "Don't be afraid. Am I in the place of God? *You intended to harm me, but God intended it for good* to accomplish what is now being done, the saving of many lives." . . . And he reassured them and spoke kindly to them. (50:17-21)

Joseph didn't say they were innocent or that they had nothing to fear. He left it to God to be their judge. What he asserted was that their harmful intentions were tools in the hands of God's good intentions—to save the entire family. What Joseph could not have seen is that the famine (bad) would draw all of Jacob's family into Egypt where they would receive food (good), and that this family would grow to become a nation (good) that would be forced into four centuries of terrible bondage in Egypt (bad). In their suffering (bad) they would cry out to God (good) and be delivered by God's mighty power through Moses (good). Their deliverance as a nation laid the foundation for understanding the bondage of sin (bad) and God's deliverance from it (good) through a Savior (good). Centuries later, the Savior was crucified (bad) and gloriously resurrected (good), and is now saving many lives right down to the present time—to you and me. This is why we can say God is at work for good in all things, good and bad, and that, trusting in God's sovereignty, we have the power to forgive those who sin against us.

Trusting God's Redeeming Love

Finally, trusting in God's redeeming love also frees us to forgive. This love hopes that the gospel of forgiveness and a new life will win our enemies over. This love desires to see our enemies converted, not condemned, so that they become a living testimony to the glory of God's mercy in Jesus Christ.

In 1987, Michael Carlucci shot Scott Everett to death. Carlucci pleaded guilty to second-degree manslaughter and was sentenced to ten years in the state penitentiary. Scott's father, Pastor Walter Everett, in spite of his own pain, wrote a letter to Carlucci and eventually visited him. Carlucci told him that, after receiving Everett's first letter, he knelt in his prison cell and asked God for forgiveness. In prison, after an hour-long discussion, the two men stood, shook hands, embraced, and cried. Pastor Everett said, "Christians won't be able to understand why Jesus came and what Jesus is all about unless we forgive."[8] This is the power of Christian love. After serving his time, Michael Carlucci decided to wed. Pastor Walter Everett performed the wedding ceremony for his son's killer.

Pastor Everett demonstrates that there is power in hoping for God's redeeming love to be glorified on the earth. This love can be so great, so lovely, so overwhelming that it empowers us to forgive those who've hurt us and love our enemies and do good to them. Pastor Everett's love reduced his son's killer to tears of repentance and faith in Christ. He proved the axiom "Mercy triumphs over judgment!" (James 2:13). Mercy (and the forgiveness inherent in it) brings greater glory to God than judgment.

So how do we push past grudges? How do we overcome evil with good? By faith in the goodness of God. The goodness of God's commands compels us to forgive. The truth that God is always working for our good frees us from bitterness. Our hope in the conquering power of the gospel not only conquers bitterness, often it overcomes the hearts of our enemies and turns their guilt into gladness.

❧

The Journey from Guilt to Gladness

Pushing past grudges is a crucial step in moving from guilt to gladness. We do that by trusting in the goodness of God. He will keep us glad of heart and free from all bitterness, hate, and revenge until we finally obtain the full measure of grace that brings eternal life.

Chapter Ten

Forgiveness Unsheathed

SERVING IN THE GREAT WORK

*I sometimes feel that I am living just as long as I
have something great to work for.*
—DIETRICH BONHOEFFER, *LETTERS AND PAPERS FROM PRISON*

❧

*We are . . . created in Christ Jesus to do good works,
which God prepared in advance for us to do.*
—EPHESIANS 2:10

Ray entered Harvard at age fifteen *as a sophomore*, graduated at nineteen, and was a medical doctor by the time he was twenty-three. Dr. Ray Hammond, an African American, is a godly brother and a friend of mine. I knew he was gifted, but until I read this information in the *Boston Globe*,[1] I didn't know he was so singularly gifted. Why? Because I know him not as a medical doctor but as the pastor of Bethel African Methodist Episcopal Church here in Boston's inner city. A few years back, when Dr. Hammond was enjoying a six-figure income as a surgeon on Cape Cod, he set it all aside and started this church in his living room with his wife and four children, living on $32,000 a year. The mayor of Boston offered him an $80,000-plus, cabinet-level post as chief of human services. He politely refused and remains pastor of the 250-member church. What compels a man of such immense talent, for whom success, prosperity, and fame are so clearly achievable, to turn to preaching and pastoring instead among the distressed neighborhoods of Boston?

Sylvia Anthony's husband died in 1987. Before he died, however, the hospital supervising his care burned a hole in his stomach, making a sick man even sicker. The hospital awarded him $90,000 for its error. Being a generous man, he gave over half of it away before he died. Sylvia used a little of it to bury her husband and the rest to house young unwed mothers needing transitional housing. She opened her home and, when that filled up, rented another. In two years she had spent almost all the money, but by then enough other people had joined in to help nurse the work along. Now called Sylvia's Haven, her endeavor was awarded fifty housing units from the government when it closed Fort Devens army base in Massachusetts. What compels a woman in her sixties, in the midst of her grief, to take the biggest chunk of money she ever saw and spend it on lost, sometimes drug-addicted and usually rebellious, young unwed mothers?

When I was a senior in high school, I came to faith in Christ and within a year every member of my family except for my father followed. My mother's new dedication to Christ helped her endure a difficult marriage and kept her well motivated to be a caring and challenging public school teacher. In the last twenty years she prayed for and encouraged the members of my family as we went into various forms of Christian service. At one point, she had a child in each time zone in the country. A couple of years ago she found herself widowed and retired. One day she called to tell me she was moving to *Russia* as a missionary! At sixty-six years old, she is bearing the harsh winters of Nizhny Novgorod (Gorky) and teaching Christian ethics and morality in the public schools to teachers, students, and their parents. Is she daft? Or is there something about experiencing the forgiveness of God that compels us into great works of love?

RECIPIENTS OF THE GOSPEL BECOME
SERVANTS OF THE GOSPEL

Ray, Sylvia, and my mother demonstrate how every recipient of the gospel becomes a servant of the gospel; it's part of the gift of grace. The apostle Paul wrote, "I became a servant of this gospel *by the gift of God's grace* given me through the working of His power. Although I am less than the least of all God's people, this gift was given to me" (Ephesians 3:7-8). The gospel calls us to repentance and faith for the forgiveness of sins, then it commissions us to a life of service. We breathe in salvation and we exhale servanthood. Serving God is an outlet for our joy in God.

> Praise be to the Lord, the God of Israel,
>> because He has come and has redeemed His people. . . .
> to rescue us from the hand of our enemies,
>> *and to enable us to serve Him without fear*
> in holiness and righteousness before Him all our days.
> (Luke 1:68,74-75)

Serving God is the way we replenish our joy in God as the years go by. "Never be lacking in zeal, but keep your spiritual fervor, serving the Lord" (Romans 12:11). It's our glad obedience to God's command. "Serve one another in love" (Galatians 5:13). It's something love compels us to do, as 1 Peter 5:2 says, "not because you must, but because you are willing, as God wants you to be; not greedy for money, but eager to serve." Servanthood is a way of life among the forgiven. Charles Swindoll calls it "the art of unselfish living."[2] That's because the new focus of our life is to love God and our neighbor.

Serving God becomes the *purpose* of our life on earth. Hebrews 9:14 declares, "How much . . . will the blood of Christ . . . cleanse our consciences from acts that lead to death, so that we may serve the living God!" We began as guilty sinners, living empty lives, and through the sanctifying power of His Spirit and belief in the truth, God washes, heals, molds, and spurs us to a place where we wake up every day of our lives with the highest of all purposes for getting out of bed. We serve the living God!

Let's return one last time to our anchor text and notice how gloriously far the gospel takes us: from being a guilty sinner to a servant of God.

Once you were alienated from God and were enemies in your minds because of your evil behavior. But now He has reconciled you by Christ's physical body through death to present you holy in His sight, without blemish and free from accusation—if you continue in your faith, established and firm, not moved from the hope held out in the gospel. This is the gospel that you heard and that has been proclaimed to every creature under heaven, *and of which I, Paul, have become a servant.* (Colossians 1:21-23)

Can the gulf between where we start and where we end be any greater? Can anything be more honoring and yet humbling than to be used as God's servant? Is anything more winsome and needed than this kind of Christian faith lived out in our neighborhood? It's this arching experience from guilt to gladness, from sinner to servant, that glorifies God's redeeming love in a suffering and evil world.

SERVING GOD MEANS FINDING SOMETHING GOOD TO DO

I asked Sylvia Anthony when she first thought about opening her home to unwed mothers. She said, "From the moment I became a Christian, I wanted to serve God; I just wasn't sure how. Then I heard about how young mothers needed places to stay in order to keep their babies, and I just knew I had to do something." Sylvia's experience of forgiveness is the Christian experience. Once our life has been secured in Christ, we naturally turn our attention to the needs of others and look for something good to do.

God has ordained for each of us something good to do. Ephesians 2:10 says, "We are . . . created in Christ Jesus to do good works, which God prepared in advance for us to do." Christ died to secure in our faith a desire to do good works. Titus 2:14 says, "[Christ] gave himself for us to redeem us from all wickedness and to purify for himself a people that are His very own, *eager to do what is good*".

OUR GOOD WORKS ARE WORKS OF FAITH

As with everything in our Christian experience, this step from guilt to gladness is one of faith. The good works we find to do are works generated from our faith. First Thessalonians 1:3 says, "We continually remember before our God and Father *your work produced by faith*, your labor prompted by love, and your endurance inspired by hope in our Lord Jesus Christ." The faith that believes Christ died for our sins also believes the work God has for us to do will produce the greatest happiness in us and bring the greatest glory to Him.

Our good works of service are definitely *not* works we do because God can't get things done without us, as if He has a need that we are meeting. God has no such need. "The God who made the world and everything in it is the Lord of heaven and earth and does not live in temples built by hands. And *He is not served by human hands, as if He needed anything*, because He himself gives all men life and breath and everything else" (Acts 17:24-25). It is certainly tempting to motivate Christian service by flattery. "God needs you. We are God's hands and feet" is a popular appeal. But God is not served by human hands! This means it's insulting and demeaning to think that we serve Him because He has no ability to do things without our help. He holds the idea up to ridicule. Psalm 50:9-15 says:

> "I have no need of a bull from your stall
>   or of goats from your pens,
> for every animal of the forest is mine,
>   and the cattle on a thousand hills.
> I know every bird in the mountains,
>   and the creatures of the field are mine.
> If I were hungry I would not tell you,
>   for the world is mine, and all that is in it.
> Do I eat the flesh of bulls
>   or drink the blood of goats?
> Sacrifice thank offerings to God,

fulfill your vows to the Most High,
and call upon me in the day of trouble;
I will deliver you, and you will honor me."

God has no need to be served; we have a need to serve. God gives me work to do in the same way I gave a paintbrush to my son when he was small. Since he loved his dad, he wanted to do what Dad did. He wanted to paint *with* Dad and climb the ladder *like* Dad and have his picture taken *beside* Dad in front of the house when it was done. Dad could have painted the house all by himself, and done it more quickly and better. But Dad enjoys his son and is pleased by the son's desire to imitate him. So being his dad, I brought him out to see what was going on and calculated the minutes till he would ask, "Can I paint too?" At first my hand overlaid his as he brushed on the paint. I taught and directed him what to do. I held him steady on the ladder.

So it is with our good works. God is working in and through us. In practice this means serving with a conscious *dependence* on God to supply the wisdom and power needed for the work and doing it with a conscious *desire* to advance the glory of God's name—not ours—in the world. First Peter 4:11 points to both of these. "If anyone serves, he should do it with the strength God provides, so that in all things God may be praised through Jesus Christ."

OUR GOOD WORKS ARE PART OF HIS GREAT WORK

The German pastor Dietrich Bonhoeffer, arrested and eventually executed for his opposition to Hitler, wrote from his cell, "I sometimes feel that I am living just as long as I have something great to work for."[3] What makes it so exciting to serve God is that we are serving in a Great Cause. Our good works are a contributing part to His Great Work.

What is God's Great Work? The Great Work is God's *global* movement to bring many people over from guilt to gladness. First Peter 2:9-10 says of us,

You are a chosen people, a royal priesthood, a holy nation, a people belonging to God, *that you may declare the praises of Him who called you out of darkness into His wonderful light.* Once you were not a people, but now you are the people of God; once you had not received mercy, but now you have received mercy.

The Great Work of God consists of Him building a nation of people, united by a personal, heartfelt experience of His forgiveness, living out a life of trust in Him, and all together declaring the praises of His glory.

A few weeks after I became a Christian at seventeen, I was sitting in church and an older gentleman stood up to lead the congregation in an evening prayer. In his prayer, he praised God for His faithfulness that he had personally experienced the past thirty years. I sat there amazed, thinking, *God, this thing You're doing in me, You've been doing it a long time now. Thirty years!* I was awakening to the reality that trusting in Christ brought me into something historic and global—something far greater than I first realized. As my faith grew I learned how great is God's Great Work.

HOW GREAT IS THE GREAT WORK?

God's Great Work was conceived before the creation of the world (Ephesians 1:4). It was first revealed when God declared to Abraham His intention to launch a global movement from guilt to gladness.

> "I will make you into a great nation
>   and I will bless you;
> I will make your name great,
>   and you will be a blessing.
> I will bless those who bless you,
>
>   and whoever curses you I will curse;
> and *all peoples on earth*
>   will be blessed through you." (Genesis 12:2-3)

Through Abraham, God would build a nation, and then through that nation God would so work that *all the peoples on earth* would be made glad of heart (blessed). Centuries later, King David, now leader of the very nation God promised to create, worshiped God in anticipation of the gladdening that would flow from Israel into the river of every nation and the rivulet of every people group in those nations.

> That your ways may be known on earth,
> your salvation among all nations.
> May the peoples praise you, O God;
> may all the peoples praise you.
> *May the nations be glad and sing for joy.* (Psalm 67:2-4)

When Jesus came, He commissioned us to serve under His own authority in the global advancement of this Great Work. He said, in Matthew 28:18-20:

> "All authority in heaven and on earth has been given to me. Therefore go and make disciples of all nations,[4] baptizing them in the name of the Father and of the Son and of the Holy Spirit, and teaching them to obey everything I have commanded you. And surely I am with you always, to the very end of the age."

We live in the shadow of the approaching completion of the Great Work. By trusting in Christ personally, we bring the Great Work one step closer to fulfillment. We advance the Great Work by the power of a godly life and the good works produced by our faith. In so doing, others move from guilt to gladness, till all of God's elect are brought over. By the time the Great Work is completed, people from every tribe and tongue on earth will gladly testify to a heartfelt experience of God's forgiveness through their faith in Jesus Christ. Revelation 7:9-10 gives us a picture of the completed work:

> After this I looked and there before me was a great multitude that no one could count, from every nation, tribe,

people and language, standing before the throne and in front of the Lamb. They were wearing white robes and were holding palm branches in their hands. And they cried out in a loud voice:

"Salvation belongs to our God
who sits on the throne,
and to the Lamb."

THE GREATEST WORLD MOVEMENT IN HISTORY

The spectacular advancement of God's Great Work is visible by tracing out the growth of the church. After Christ ascended, the entire church for the most part could fit into a single room. In Acts 1:12-14 we read that the disciples of Jesus gathered for prayer in an upper room "along with the women and Mary the mother of Jesus, and with His brothers." By the end of their lives, the movement had penetrated the major cites of the known world. By A.D. 100 Christians constituted a tiny 0.5 percent of the world population. It took another 1,400 years to hit the 1 percent mark (circa 1430), but it took only 360 years to hit 2 percent of the world population (1790) and only 150 years to move to 3 percent, which occurred around 1940. In the last 50 years we have grown to 11 percent of the world population, gaining a percentage point every 2 to 3 years![5]

Ralph Winter writes, "Despite the rapid increase of world population, Christianity is simply growing faster than any other global religion when what is measured is its most relevant type of growth—the growth of committed adherents."[6] According to the best and most conservative estimates, 82,000 people come to Christ every day![7] In China, 23,000 are added daily. In Africa, 16,000. More people have turned to Christ in the last decade from the Muslim world than in the last millennium. Why is this happening? Because Christ said, "This gospel . . . will be preached in the whole world as a testimony to all nations, and then the end will come" (Matthew 24:14). To this declaration of purpose, He swore, "I will build my church, and the gates of hell will not overcome it" (Matthew 16:18, margin).

That doesn't mean that there is no resistance. It means there is no successful resistance. The gates of hell resist! But they don't overcome. As we work to relieve suffering, the gospel wins hearts. When we are called to endure suffering, the gospel wins still more hearts!

The Great Work of the gospel has advanced in spite of the steady and sometimes deadly opposition it has faced. According to David Barrett, author of the *World Christian Encyclopedia*, more people have suffered imprisonment, torture, and death for their service to the gospel in the last hundred years than in all centuries put together. In Herbert Schlossberg's aptly named book *Called to Suffer, Called to Triumph*, he explores the terrible opposition Christians have faced in China, for example. The Cultural Revolution (1966-1976) was especially hard on the church, with Christianity equated with foreign and anti-communist ways.

✗ He tells us about Pastor Kwan Ying. In 1979, Ying climbed down a train in Beijing to greet his family. "My heart pounded as I spied my family walking my way . . . and then right past me. They hadn't recognized me. And no wonder—it had been fifteen years since we had seen each other." Kwan spent twenty-one years in prison for being a Christian and refusing to stop acting like one. But during that time, what happened? After the Cultural Revolution, information gradually seeped out that showed astonishing vitality in the repressed church, so that best estimates put the number of believers in China at over 50 million.[8] That represents a lot of glad hearts. After seventy years of communism, in which God was "deleted" from the minds of the people, the wall fell, and behold, 36 percent of Russia was Christian. It had five times the membership of the Communist Party. The stories of God's Great Work, Earle Cairns said, form "an endless line of splendor."[9]

The conquering power of the gospel has faced as much danger from within the church as from without. Moral and theological corruption has done much to scandalize the gospel and impede its progress in the hearts of men and women. The darkest moment of church history came when we perverted the gospel and tried to advance it by the sword rather than the winsome power of good works. The sad effects of the Crusades linger to this day. Even so, God brought reform and renewal, as He constantly does, so that the Great Work of bringing people from guilt to gladness is propelled forward.

HOW DO I FIND MY PART IN THE GREAT WORK?

The answer to this question is not as hard as you might think. The Great Work boils down in practice to doing the works that *love* calls us to do. The apostle Paul called it "your labor prompted by love" (1 Thessalonians 1:3). Your part in the Great Work is what God's love at work in you prompts you to do. If you will live in the love of God, He will lead you through the promptings of love to many good works of service.

Jesus told the parable of the good Samaritan to illustrate how our part in the Great Work is fulfilled by simply obeying the promptings of love. Luke 10:25-37 says the Samaritan saw a man beaten and left for dead. He was able to fulfill the law of God by simply following the law of love. He picked the man up, bandaged his wounds, took him to an inn, and paid for his care. Ralph Waldo Emerson said, "Give all to love, obey thy heart."[10] This is the biblical pattern, and it has worked as a guide for serving in the Great Work of God for centuries.

The law of love prompted the Hebrew midwives to rescue babies from death in Pharaoh's day (Exodus 1:16-20). Obadiah provided food and shelter for a hundred prophets in the days of Jezebel (1 Kings 18:4). Psalm 82:3-4 says,

> Defend the cause of the weak and fatherless;
>   maintain the rights of the poor and oppressed.
> Rescue the weak and needy;
>   deliver them from the hand of the wicked.

Why? It's the law of love.

Where the law of love is obeyed, Matthew 25:35-36 says, the sick are cared for, not euthanized. The imprisoned are visited, not left to despair in their guilt. The immigrant is assisted, not despised. The thirsty are given a glass of water. Isn't it amazing that fetching water can be one of the good works God has prepared in advance that we should do? Love should lead some of us men to befriend the neighbor boy who has no dad. Love should lead some to check in on the elderly woman who's lost her husband and perhaps fix her faucet.

Love is creative in its good works. Love invented the piggy bank! It was originally created by mission societies as a fundraising method to provide missionaries in China with funds for buying piglets. And why were the missionaries there? Love prompted them to leave their own neighborhood and adopt a new one so that the gladness of the gospel could spread to the nations. Love led the early missionaries to Africa to pack their belongings in *coffins* because they had such a short life expectancy. Tropical diseases generally claimed their lives within a year of arriving on the mission field. Medical missions started in an effort to prolong the life of missionaries. Why? Because we loved them and the people they went to serve. Love has started many schools. Eighty-five percent of the schools in Africa today were started by Christians.[11] What has happened as a result? In 1900, Africa was 4 percent Christian. Today 40 percent of the people of Africa identify themselves as Christian. Good works, prompted by love, produce a Great Work.

Dr. Robertson McQuilken was doing a good work. He was the president of Columbia Bible College and Seminary in Columbia, South Carolina. This school has a worldwide ministry and a 10 million dollar budget. In 1990 his wife was stricken with Alzheimer's disease. For several years, with extra help, he was able to serve both the college and his wife. But the law of love told him when it was time to resign his highly respected worldwide ministry to care for his wife through "her brave descent into oblivion."

When the time came, the decision was firm. It took no great calculation. It was a matter of integrity. Had I not promised, 42 years before, "in sickness and in health . . . till death do us part"?

This was no grim duty to which I was stoically resigned, however. It was only fair. She had, after all, cared for me for almost four decades with marvelous devotion; now it was my turn. And such a partner she was! If I took care of her for 40 years, I would never be out of her debt. . . .

Resignation was painful; but the right path was not difficult to discern.[12]

Do you see how love never fails? It's a sure guide to doing the will of God. It may lead some of us to pack our mittens and head for Moscow. It may lead some to open their spare bedroom to an unwed mother in pregnancy distress. It may lead a surgeon to the city. But it will lead all of us who love Jesus and long for His appearing to say with Mary, "I am the Lord's servant" (Luke 1:38).

The Journey from Guilt to Gladness

Serving God, by serving in His Great Work of bringing the gospel's love, truth, and mercy to the world around us, is the Christian's fountain of youth. It keeps us ever young in the gladness of God and ever hopeful for the spread of His glory.

AN EPILOGUE

As we have seen, the Christian experience of God's forgiveness takes us far beyond our need for forgiveness. It serves as a foundation for living out the Christian experience of "God with us." The more clear and satisfying our heartfelt experience of God's forgiveness is, the more firmly and boldly will we live out the call of God on our lives, no matter the cost or difficulty. This is as it should be. Logic says, and the Christian mind agrees, "He who did not spare His own Son, but gave Him up for us all—how will He not also, along with Him, graciously give us all things?" (Romans 8:32). Do you see how our heartfelt experience of God's forgiveness is rock-solid evidence that God can be trusted for everything else we need to make us truly and eternally glad of heart? Past grace is the torchbearer of future grace.[13]

Since this is the case, we must never, never, never give up trusting God no matter how hard life is or how discouraged we are by our frailties and incompleteness. Instead, we are called to rejoice in the ongoing work of the grace of God and look forward to its completion. This was Paul's prayer and hope for all who believe.

> In my prayers for all of you, I always pray with *joy*
> because of your partnership in the gospel from the first
> day until now, being confident of this, that He who began
> a good work in you will carry it on to completion until
> the day of Christ Jesus. (Philippians 1:4-6,)

"The day of Jesus Christ" is something that all Christians long for. It signals the *completion* of the war against our flesh, the world, and the Devil and the *consummation* of our happiness in the holiness of God. Hold fast to this hope with me and millions of other Christians, and hold it gladly! It is the hope of glory.

Notes

Chapter One

1. These pregnancy resource centers specialize in reaching young women in pregnancy distress, especially those considering abortion due to lack of information or resources. Called *A Woman's Concern*, we're dedicated to reducing teen pregnancy and abortion and increasing abstinence-based relationships and intact, two-parent families. For more information write: *A Woman's Concern*, 1876A Dorchester Ave., Boston, MA 02124.
2. In 1973, Josh McDowell came to my hometown of DeKalb, Illinois, to speak at Northern Illinois University. I was a senior in high school and a brand-new Christian. He gave a lecture entitled "Maximum Sex." He instilled in me a biblical vision for abstinence until marriage and faithfulness within marriage. I owe him a debt of gratitude, for surely I would have fallen into the trap soon enough, apart from this grace.
3. Josh McDowell, *Sex, Guilt, and Forgiveness* (Wheaton, Ill.: Tyndale, 1990), p. 9.
4. Fyodor Dostoyevsky, *The Brothers Karamazov*, trans. Constance Garnett (New York: New American Library, 1957), pt. 2, bk. 4, p. 226.
5. Arnold Dallimore, *C. H. Spurgeon* (Chicago: Moody, 1984), pp. 17-18.
6. Henri Nouwen, as quoted by Bob Benson, and Michael W. Benson, *Disciplines of the Inner Life* (Waco, Tex.: Word, 1985), p. 30.

Chapter Two

1. Plutarch, *Lives, Demetrius*, sec. 1.
2. O. Hallesby, *Conscience*, trans. C. J. Carlsen (London: Intervarsity Fellowship, 1950), p. 9.

3. In some modern hymnals, the word *worm* has been replaced with *sinners.* I suspect that this is because *worm* runs contrary to contemporary theories on self-esteem.
4. George MacDonald, *The Gift of the Child Christ: Fairytales and Stories for the Childlike*, vol. 1 (Grand Rapids, Mich.: Eerdmans, 1973), p. 202.
5. Frederick Buechner, as quoted by Larry Crabb, *Men and Women: Enjoying the Difference* (Grand Rapids, Mich.: Zondervan, 1991), p. 25.
6. Larry Crabb, at a conference I attended, illustrated the problem of self-centeredness in marriage, saying, "We got two ticks here and no dog!"
7. C. S. Lewis, *Surprised by Joy* (New York: Harcourt, Brace & World, 1955), p. 226.
8. H. R. Mackintosh, *The Christian Experience of Forgiveness* (London: Nisbet & Co., 1927), p. 9.
9. Charles Spurgeon, *The Early Years*, ed. Iain Murray (London: Banner of Truth, 1962), p. 59.
10. Lewis, p. 227.
11. Lewis, p. 229.

Chapter Three
1. Our conscience, too, bears witness to the reality of God's wrath. As our anchor text says, "Once you were alienated from God and were *enemies in your minds* because of your evil behavior" (Colossians 1:21,). Apart from admitting our fault and need for forgiveness, all we can do is argue that our conscience is ill informed and shoot it if it won't shut up. Evil has a way of forming its own support groups, and we will need to find one if we are going to keep our conscience buried.
2. C. S. Lewis, *The Problem of Pain* (New York: Macmillan, 1962), p. 95. Lewis used this metaphor in reference to what pain does to us. He said, "No doubt Pain as God's megaphone is a terrible instrument; it may lead to final and unrepented rebellion. But it gives the only opportunity the bad man can have for amendment. It removes the veil; it plants the flag of truth within the fortress of a rebel soul." The wrath of God, as revealed in the Bible, involves pain beyond anything of this world and as such, his warnings about it have the same effect on the soul as general pain. We will tremble before so great a God or defy Him all the more.
3. Robert Murray McCheyne, "God's Rectitude in Future Punishment," in *Sermons of Robert Murray McCheyne* (Edinburgh: Banner of Truth Trust, 1961), p. 177. McCheyne was a vibrant young preacher in England who died at the age of twentyy-nine in 1843.
4. This example raises the question, Are there degrees of sin? Aren't some sins worse than others? Isn't Vera's murder worse than my stealing? The answer appears to be yes in one sense, and no in another. All sin is the same and yet different in the sense that acorns and oak trees are the same and yet different. All sin, and each sin, from the slightest to the greatest, is a no-confidence vote in the goodness and trustworthiness of God. As James said, "You want something but don't get it. You kill and covet, but you cannot have what you want. . . . You do not have, because you do not

ask God" (4:2). We argue, fight, and destroy to get what we want because we don't think God will provide it. We steal hats for the same reason. In this sense there is no difference between murder and murmuring; they are different *sins* that point to one eternally sinful sin: believing God is not trustworthy to be my very great delight! Murmuring is God-hatred in the acorn stage. Murder is God-hatred in the oak tree stage.

Jesus taught us that all sins are the same in this sense when He said in Matthew 5:21-22,

"You have heard that it was said to the people long ago, 'Do not murder, and anyone who murders will be subject to judgment.' But I tell you that anyone who is angry with his brother will be subject to judgment. Again, anyone who says to his brother, 'Raca,' is answerable to the Sanhedrin. But anyone who says, 'You fool!' will be in danger of the fire of hell."

The reason that name calling is a sin worthy of the fire of hell is because it's really the same hatred and defiance that is found in murder, which we see more clearly as a wickedness rightly to be condemned. It's also true that calling a man a jerk is murder in the acorn stage. While we minimize our sin, Jesus exposes the depth of sinfulness in each of our sins. Each of us will have to decide whether he is guilty of inflating our evil or we are guilty of minimizing it. Jesus takes the position that my name calling contains within it an evil so great that it deserves the fire of hell.

There certainly are degrees of sin, though, in terms of the pain and devastation it causes. An acorn and an oak tree may be the same in one sense, but I would very much prefer an acorn to fall on my head than an oak tree. I would certainly prefer someone to call me a jerk than to shoot me. There are degrees of maturity in evil. The more understanding we have of a moral obligation, the more evil it is to defy that obligation. So murder reflects a greater hardness of heart against the glory of God, because people generally know the obligation not to kill. In our courts, our sense of justice causes us to give different penalties depending on the degree of damage the act causes our fellow man or the degree of defiance against the social good it reflects, or the degree of moral light the accused had. In this sense there are degrees of sin. For speeding we get a ticket. For drunk driving we get jail time, especially if someone else is hurt or killed. For running down the boss because he fired us, we get life in prison or the death penalty. The greater the degree of defiance and rebellion, the greater punishment justice demands. The same is true of everlasting punishment. God judges the defacement of His glory by the amount of light (sense of moral duty) a person has received (Romans 2:12-24). For examples, see Matthew 10:15, 11:20-24, Luke 12:47-48, John 19:11.

5. W. G. T. Shedd, *The Doctrine of Eternal Punishment* (Edinburg: Banner of Truth Trust, 1986), pp. 12-13.

6. There are some people who dispute that hell is eternal and penal in nature. They argue that *eternal punishment* doesn't mean punishment that is eter-

nal. They suggest that at some point the wicked cease to exist. I fear this is wishful thinking. In Matthew 25:46, Jesus clearly draws an evenhanded picture; either we will be judged worthy to receive eternal life or eternal punishment. The word *eternal* is applied to both, and I've never read anyone argue that eternal life doesn't mean being alive in God's presence forever. In addition, the punishment of hell, Jesus says elsewhere, is "where the fire never goes out" (Mark 9:43) and the "worm does not die. . .and the fire is not quenched" (Mark 9:48). Further indication that God's wrath, according to Jesus, does not involve being annihilated at some point, where we cease to exist, is found in the damnation of Judas. "Woe to that man who betrays the Son of Man! It would be better for him if he had not been born" (Matthew 26:24). I take this to mean that Judas would welcome a state of nonexistence, like he had before he was born, but will not find it. For further study, see Robert Peterson, *Hell on Trial* (Phillipsburg, N.J.: P & R Publishing, 1995).

7. Moral goodness, according to the Bible, as we will learn, refers to what we do out of our personal relationship to God, through our faith in Christ, for the glory of His name (Romans 14:6; Acts 17:31).

Chapter Four

1. Charles Simeon, as quoted by John Stott in *Evangelical Preaching: An Anthology of Sermons by Charles Simeon* (Portland, Oreg.: Multnomah, 1986), p. xxxv.
2. Søren Kierkegaard, *Fear and Trembling and the Sickness unto Death*, trans. Walter Lowrie (Princeton, N.J.: Princeton University Press, First PP Edition, 1968), p. 154. This death, Kierkegaard went on to describe, is *eternal* in nature.

> Thus it is that despair, this sickness in the self, is the sickness unto death. The despairing man is mortally ill. In an entirely different sense than can appropriately be said of any disease, we may say that the sickness has attacked the noblest part; and yet the man cannot die. Death is not the last phase of the sickness, but death is *continually* the last. To be delivered from this sickness by death is an impossibility, for the sickness and its torment . . . and death consist in not being able to die.

This is a stunning description of the torments of hell.

3. Electronic mail sent to me, used by permission.
4. Quoted from Peter Masters, *Men of Destiny*, rev. ed. (London: Wakeman Trust, 1989), p. 91.
5. Masters, p. 96.
6. Daniel P. Fuller, *The Unity of the Bible* (Grand Rapids, Mich.: Zondervan, 1992), p. 196.

Chapter Five

1. The very first promise of a coming rescuer was given in Genesis 3:15.

200

2. Jesus did not come to rescue everybody, or everybody would be rescued through His complete work on the cross. He came to "save *His people* from their sins" (Matthew 1:21). "His people" are those who repent and put their faith in Him.

> "The Redeemer will come to Zion,
> to those in Jacob who repent of their sins," declares
> the LORD. (Isaiah 59:20; see also Galatians 3:26)

When the angels appeared to the shepherds, they shouted,

> Glory to God in the highest,
> and on earth peace to men on whom His favor rests.
> (Luke 2:14)

His peace is not on everyone, but on those on whom His favor rests. His favor rests, as we learned in the last chapter, on those who repent and put their hope in God. He fiercely opposes the rest. Jesus used the metaphor of the shepherd and the sheep to explain the scope of His mission. The shepherd "calls his own sheep by name and leads them out. . . . His sheep follow him because they know his voice" (John 10:3-4). Then He applied this to Himself and the people He came to rescue. "I am the good shepherd; I know my sheep and my sheep know me—just as the Father knows me and I know the Father—and I lay down my life for the sheep" (10:14-15). If you ask who are His sheep, it's those who *hear His voice and follow Him.* The rest, who refuse His call, are not His sheep and will remain condemned for their guilt. When Jesus was about to lay down His life on the cross, He prayed for those He came to rescue. It isn't everybody in the whole world. "I am not praying for the world, but *for those you have given me,* for they are yours" (John 17:9). When you ask who the Father has *given* to the Son to purchase forgiveness for and give eternal life, the answer again is not everybody, but those who *believe,* shown by their *obedience* to God's Word. "They were yours; you gave them to me and they have *obeyed* your word. . . . They knew with certainty that I came from you, and they *believed*" (John 17:6,8). The biblical and theological word for those included in Christ's rescue mission is the *elect* (Matthew 24:22-31, Romans 11:7, 2 Timothy 2:10). The distinguishing mark of the elect is *faith* in Christ—repentant, obedient, persevering, joyful faith. We grow in confidence that we are among the elect as we grow in this faith, for that is how the elect *prove* they are the elect (2 Peter 1:3-11, especially verse 10).

3. God desires to make His mercy the apex of His own glory in the eyes of all creation. It's the ultimate reason for the creation of the world and the plan of redemption. Why did God create a world of sin and death, redemption and resurrection? Dana Olson, in his ordination paper many years ago opened my eyes,

> Prior to creation God had no means of revealing one pinnacle attribute of His glory, mercy. While He could within the fellowship of the Trinity express love and maintain justice, mercy inherently

201

NOTES

requires some injustice or inadequacy before loving-kindness can be expressed in forgiveness. For this reason God set in motion redemptive history—to manifest His glory by revealing this very capacity to redeem, mercy. [Dana Olson, unpublished ordination paper, ps. 1-2. Used by permission.]

God wants to reveal the richness of His mercy "to the praise of His glory" (Ephesians 1:6). This is precisely the reasoning of Romans 9:22-23. "What if God, choosing to show His wrath and make His power known, bore with great patience the objects of His wrath—prepared for destruction? What if He did this *to make the riches of His glory known to the objects of His mercy*, whom He prepared in advance for glory?" In His final judgment God will display the power of His wrath. But God could not demonstrate His capacity for mercy apart from ordaining a world of sin and a way for redemption. He endures with great patience the impenitent, so that He can magnify His all-glorious mercy in the eyes of those who put their hope in Him! (See also Titus 3:5 and 1 Peter 2:9-10).
4. Blaise Pascal, *The Mind on Fire: The Anthology of the Writings of Blaise Pascal*, ed. James M. Houston (Portland, Oreg.: Multnomah, 1989), p. 164.
5. Jonathan Edwards, "The Excellency of Christ," in *The Works of Jonathan Edwards*, vol. 1 (Edinburgh: Banner of Truth Trust, 1976), p. 687.

Chapter Six
1. Lance Gay, "Auschwitz Survivors Pay Tribute to Victims," *Boston Herald*, January 27, 1995, p. 3. Note: Some may think such a prayer is cold or wicked. It might be. Such prayers can be. But I think Dr. Wiesel's prayer is rooted in a deep sense of divine justice. He knows that God must act justly or show a great contempt for the people He created in His image that were so degraded and so many slaughtered, and in some way, to some degree, he senses God's glory demeaned here. We find similar prayers in the Bible. For example, Jeremiah prayed for relief against all his oppressors:

> You know, O LORD,
>   all their plots against me.
> Do not forgive their crimes
>   or blot out their sins from your sight. (Jeremiah 18:23)

2. Martin Hengel, *Crucifixion*, trans. John Bowden (Philadelphia: Fortress, 1977), pp. 22, 25.
3. Jacqueline Syrup Bergan and S. Marie Schwan, *Forgiveness: A Guide for Prayer* (Winona, Minn.: Saint Mary's Press, 1985), pp. 15-16.
4. How is it that such a short though intense period of suffering can fully pay the eternal debt I owe for my evil behavior? How can three days of suffering pay an eternity of condemnation for *all* of God's people? I don't know. My mind overheats when I try to grasp it from that angle. But I do know the suffering Christ endured as our complete atonement did not start with His betrayal and arrest, crucifixion and burial. It was only consummated there.

From the moment Christ was conceived of the virgin Mary, He suffered the immeasurable loss of glory and took up our humiliation and shame.

> Being in very nature God,
> [He] did not consider equality with God some
> thing to be grasped,
> *but made himself nothing,*
> *taking on the nature of a servant,*
> being made in human likeness. (Philippians 2:6-7)

Contemplate the painful loss of glory, majesty, power, and union He enjoyed with the Father. In being born He died to it all and became *nothing* and a *servant* to sinful man.

Imagine the pain of losing all your human abilities and liberties if one day you humbled yourself to be a poodle. The humiliation and frustration would be intense and immediate. Now you can't see anything above two feet. You can't lift anything except by your mouth. You can't hold a pen to write a love letter. You can't hold a nail to build a house. You can't cook a Thanksgiving meal. You now eat hard, dry cereal or mushy, canned mystery meat every day. You drink only water, which you must lap with your tongue. You must sleep in the corner, moan at the door whenever you have to relieve yourself, and then do it outside in the open. Every time you want to say something, the same sound comes out of your mouth more or less. And your essential value and admiration come in direct proportion to how well you meet the needs of humans, as their servant. In the same way, only infinitely greater in degree, Christ suffered the loss of all His glory as God in humbling Himself to be a man and then a servant to sinful men.

Then His suffering increased. He suffered poverty and lack of comfort from the moment He was born in a cowshed (Luke 2:7). He was hunted for destruction by Herod, so that His parents had to take Him and flee to Egypt. He suffered the loss of all His divine prerogatives and grew up as a simple carpenter, making His living "by the sweat of [His] brow" (Genesis 3:19).

When He did publicly show His glory, He suffered the intense shame and humiliation of being judged a glutton and a drunkard (Matthew 11:19). We all know how hard it is to endure a false accusation! Consider how much worse it was for Christ. He is all Truth, yet He was called a deceiver (John 7:12). He possessed the mind of God, but was considered a madman (John 10:20). If you can sense how painful this was to endure, remember that the charge did not come from His enemies only. His own family thought He was "out of his mind" (Mark 3:21).

Christ was accused of being demonic and a blasphemer of the very God whose name He came to glorify (Luke 5:21). Christ suffered this reproach everywhere He went, and even survived numerous assassination attempts (Matthew 2:13, 12:14, 26:4). Finally, He was betrayed by one He befriended for three years and sold to His assassins for thirty pieces of gold, the price of a slave (Mark 14:41).

Having all His divine glory rejected, He then suffered the loss of His dignity as a man—stripped naked, spit upon, degraded, and mocked. Finally, He suffered the cross. But take note that it was not the same kind of death that martyrs suffer. Martyrs face death with the peace of God coursing through their veins, strengthening their hearts. When Stephen was seized and falsely accused, he proclaimed the faith with such presence of God that even his judges saw that he had the "face of an angel" (Acts 6:15). He suffered the stones in peace. So have thousands of others suffered and died under the hatred of men. But Christ suffered both the hatred of men and the wrath of God in His death. His heart and soul suffered the loss of God's friendship, even as His body was tortured. He endured the public humiliation throughout His life with the comfort that the Father was always with Him. But not on the cross. There He suffered the loss of peace with God and took up His enmity (our enmity).

> All my bones are out of joint.
> My heart has turned to wax;
>   it has melted away within me. (Psalm 22:14)

I can't quantify mathematically how Christ pays the complete punishment of all who would hope in Him, but I see Him paying it from the start, bearing our shame as well as our punishment.

5. The demand for faithfulness sounds to many in the modern church like a departure from the truth that salvation is the free gift of God. It sounds to them as if works of human effort rather than faith alone then becomes the basis of God's grace; and grace that is merited is no longer grace. While it is true that God's grace is free and unmerited, the New Testament does not see faithfulness as a work of human merit but rather a consistent trust in God's meritorious work on our behalf. Faithfulness is *faith* exercising its dependence and trust in God on a daily basis. Indeed, anything other than faithfulness is an expression of removing one's confidence in God and trusting in something else. That is why faithfulness is demanded throughout Scripture as the sign of faith that secures salvation. Jesus said, "All men will hate you because of me, but *he who stands firm to the end will be saved*" (Mark 13:13). 2 Timothy 2:12 says, "*If we endure*, we will also reign with Him. If we disown Him, He will also disown us." The condition for reigning with Christ is faithfulness to Christ. Therefore Hebrews 3:12-14 warns us, "See to it, brothers, that none of you has a sinful, unbelieving heart that turns away from the living God. But encourage one another daily, as long as it is called Today, so that none of you may be hardened by sin's deceitfulness. *We come to share in Christ if we hold firmly till the end the confidence we had at first.*"

The necessity for persevering faith is a truth largely lost in the church today. In its place is a biblically truncated view that reduces faith to some puntiliar act of "believing" that is divorced from living a life of slowing maturing dependence and trust in God and His will. In some groups this truncated faith is then connected to all the promises of heaven so that people who live with no passion for God and His glory are "assured of their eternal security" in spite of all the warnings of Scripture that "those who live according to the flesh will die" (Romans 8:13), simply because at some point in their earlier life they made a "decision." But Scripture sees saving faith as a *life-changing* gift of God. Through faith, God justifies (Romans 5:1), then sanctifies (2 Thessalonians 2:13) and eventually glorifies (Colossians 1:22-23) each recipient of His grace. Therefore enduring faith is necessary for salvation, and experiencing it is a sign of the enduring work of the grace of God, not human effort (Philippians 1:3-6; 1 Corinthians 1:8-9). Even Paul looked for this in himself as the basis for his hope for salvation (Philippians 3:10-11; 1 Corinthians 9:25-27; 2 Timothy 4:7).

God preserves His elect for all eternity *by giving them* a persevering faith. Therefore the necessity of faithfulness doesn't make faith any less a gift from God, it defines the kind of faith that God gives us as His gift and helps us distinguish it from false forms of faith that are found in human experience (See John 2:23-24; Matthew 13:21, James 2:14 for examples of people who had faith but not the kind that is saving in nature).

6. Archimedes, *Pappus of Alexandria*, Collection, bk. 7, prop. 10, sec. 11.

Chapter Seven

1. In contemporary psychology, there is a great emphasis on distinguishing between guilt and shame. When I do something bad I feel guilty. When I feel I *am* bad, that is shame. I don't follow this line of thinking. The premise that accompanies it is that shame is always misplaced. The therapist's goal is to persuade the patient that "you are not bad, what you did was bad." I don't think most people can hold the two separate except through a lot of mind games. What I do is a reflection of who I am. If I am doing bad, it's a sign that something is really wrong with *me* that must be changed. The Bible teaches us that we are by nature sinners and that is why we sin. I use shame and guilt to reflect a subtle difference rather than a big difference. Guilt is more judicial, more the voice of conscience as an objective witness that we have done wrong. Shame is more the emotional pain we suffer because of our sin.

2. This is the lesson of Romans 5:3. "We also rejoice in our sufferings, because we know that suffering produces perseverance; perseverance, character; and character, hope." Also James 1:2-4 says, "Consider it pure joy, my brothers, whenever you face trials of many kinds, because you know that the testing of your faith develops perseverance. Perseverance must finish its work so that you may be mature and complete, not lacking in anything."

3. Some people use the term *limited atonement* to mean that Christ paid the full penalty for *some* people (those who believe). While this may be true, it confuses more than clarifies. I use the term *complete atonement* to put the emphasis where I think Scripture does, that Christ endured *all* the punishment of *all* who believe. God honors all who call to Him in faith with complete forgiveness. "*Everyone* who calls on the name of the Lord will be saved" (Acts 2:21). See chapter 5, footnote two for more.

4. This is Daniel Fuller's translation of Romans 5:1. See Daniel Fuller, *The Unity of the Bible* (Grand Rapids, Mich.: Zondervan, 1992), p. 275.

5. Numbers 13–14 provides a clear example of how defiant and persistent unbelief can cloak itself in the humble language of repentance. God prepared Israel to take the Promised Land. Joshua and Caleb were ready to obey, but the rest were afraid and grumbled. In a sad way, God answered their prayers and refused to take them into the land. Instead they would live in the wilderness for forty years till they all died and the next generation would trust Him for victory. "When Moses reported this to all the Israelites, they mourned bitterly" (14:39). This certainly sounds like godly sorrow. They said, "We have sinned. . . . We will go up to the place the LORD promised" (14:40). This sounds like true repentance. But it wasn't. It was another example of continued defiance. They refused to humbly accept God's judgment on them. Moses said, "Why are you disobeying the LORD's command? This will not succeed! Do not go up, because the LORD is not with you. You will be defeated by your enemies" (14:41-42). They went up anyway, and got whipped. God told them to go and they said no. God told them not to go and they said they would anyway. Defiant unbelief *can* cloak itself in tears of regret. But where God's judgment is not yielded to as the best judgment, all else is defiance and unbelief, no matter how humble it sounds.

6. Corrie ten Boom and Jamie Buckingham, *Tramp for the Lord* (Old Tappan, N.J.: Revell, 1974), p. 108.

Chapter Eight

1. Larry Crabb, *Men and Women: Enjoying the Difference* (Grand Rapids, Mich.: Zondervan, 1991), p. 90.

2. Crabb, p. 91.

3. John Piper, *Desiring God* (Portland, Oreg.: Multnomah, 1986), p. 41.

4. Some people suggest that it's a little mercenary to worship God for the good things He does for us. They direct us to love God and worship Him for Himself alone, and not for His benefits to us. There's a long tradition in the mystics that encourages this, but I'm persuaded that it's wrong. I do concede that it sounds very spiritual though. For example, Albert Day writes in his book *An Autobiography of Prayer*,

> We never really adore Him, until we arrive at the moment when we worship Him for what He is in Himself, apart from any consideration of the impact of His Divine Selfhood upon our desires and our welfare. Then we love Him for Himself alone. Then we adore Him, regardless of whether any personal benefit is in anticipation or not. . . . That is pure adoration. Nothing less is worthy of the name. (As quoted by Bob Benson and Michael W. Benson, *Disciplines of the Inner Life* [Waco, Tex.: Word, 1985], p. 53.)

Just at the practical level, this advice demands a herculean effort of mind control. I find it impossible to say, "I love You, God, You are so great!" without my mind recalling some of the great works God has done for *my* benefit. But more important, this advice is nowhere encouraged or demonstrated in the Bible. Instead, what we find are multiple examples that encourage us to love God *for His benefits.* Psalm 103:2 even tells us to make sure *not* to forget His benefits as we praise His name.

Praise the LORD, O my soul,
and forget not all His benefits.

Isaiah 61:10 calls to mind God's benefits as fuel for worship.

I delight greatly in the LORD;
my soul rejoices in my God.
For He has clothed me with garments of salvation
and arrayed me in a robe of righteousness.

This isn't mercenary. It's God-glorifying.

If my son Elliot comes up to me and says, "Papa, I love you, but it isn't because you feed me or teach me or play catch with me. I love you, but not because you ran me to the hospital when I got sick and came to my defense when that guy in the park tried to lure me into his car that day. I love you just because of who you are." I would not feel honored by this. I'm his *father.* That is who I am. As his father, I'm glorified in his dependence on me as a provider and protector. Let him praise me all he wants for the great things I've done for him, and I'll be glorified as his father. So God is to be praised and glorified as our Father—our provider, the giver of good gifts. That's why no place in the Bible is this sort of super-spirituality encouraged. Worship the Lord for the beauty of His character but know that God wants to show His character by being the giver of good gifts.

5. Edward Taylor, "Should I With Silver Tools Delve Through The Hill," from *The Mentor Book of Major American Poets* edited by Williams & Honig (New York, NY: New American Library, 1962), p. 42.

6. Because of the deceitfulness of sin, and our natural ability to deceive ourselves we are called to examine ourselves to see whether or not we are in the faith (2 Corinthians 13:5; 2 Peter 1:10). We are to look for the *evidence* of saving faith which is a glad heart to obey. We prove our status as children of God by the fruit of faithful obedience. See John 14:21; Romans 8:13; 1 Corinthians 6:9-11; Galatians 5:16-25; 1 John 1:5-7; 3:4-10.

Chapter Nine

1. The phrase, "finally obtaining the full measure of grace that brings eternal life" will be confusing and objectionable to some people. But the point that I am trying to establish in this chapter is that forgiving others is *necessary* for final salvation. I am trying to be faithful to Matthew 6:14-15 which says, "If you forgive men when they sin against you, your heavenly Father will also forgive you. But if you do not forgive men their sins, your Father will not forgive your sins." This is a *conditional* promise of the grace of God, and as such, is largely confusing to the modern ear. John Piper wrote, "The biblical concept of unmerited, *conditional* grace is nearly unintelligible to many contemporary Christians who assume that *unconditionality* is the essence of all grace. To be sure, there is unconditional grace. And it is the glorious

foundation of all else in the Christian life. But there is also *conditional* grace. For most people who breathe the popular air of grace and compassion today, *conditional grace* sounds like an oxymoron—like heavy feathers. So, for example, when, people hear the promise of James 4:6, that God "gives grace *to the humble*," many have a hard time thinking about a grace that is conditional upon humility." (John Piper, *Future Grace*, p. 11-12)

And yet, there are numerous examples of conditional grace in Scripture (see John 14:21; Luke 1:50; Hebrews 12:14; 1 John 1:7). The one we are owing up to in this chapter is the necessity of a forgiving heart. That does not mean we are meriting our salvation. Indeed, the actions that flow from a forgiving heart demonstrate that we have *faith* in God. How so? By forgiving, we demonstrate a *rejection* of human effort to bring about justice and vindication and show that we are trusting and depending on God's promise which says, "It is mine to avenge; I will repay" (Deuteronomy 32:35; Romans 12:19). That's why God can demand us to forgive those who've victimized us, because forgiveness is faith in God expressing itself—and this faith is what connects us to the gift of forgiveness and eternal life.

I understand all the conditions of grace this way, as various expressions of faith in God. The love for God required in John 14:21 is the work of God's grace according to Deuteronomy 30:6. Obedience to the will of God is one of the conditions of grace (Matthew 7:21), but it is also an expression of faith in the sanctifying power of God (Philippians 2:13). Even the condition of "doing good" (Romans 2:7) is really an expression of faith according to James 2:14-19. As James said, "Show me your faith without deeds, and I will show you my faith by what I do" (2:18).

Therefore, John Piper is right to help us see that, "Conditional grace is not earned grace. It is not merited. 'Earned grace' is an oxymoron. Grace cannot be earned. The very meaning of grace is that the one receiving the grace does not deserve it—has not earned it. If a philanthropist pays $80,000 for your college education on the condition that you graduate from high school, you have not earned the gift, but you have met a condition. It is possible to meet a condition for receiving grace and yet not earn grace. Conditional grace does not mean earned grace. How can this be? The part of the answer that needs to be said here is that when God's grace is based on a condition, that condition is also a work of God's grace. This guarantees the absolute freeness of grace. The philanthropist mentioned above may even become the personal tutor for a failing high school student to insure that he does get his diploma and so meets the condition for the $80,000 grant." (*Future Grace*, pp. 78-79)

In regard to the need to forgive others, God not only demands it, but works in our hearts to help us meet the condition of forgiving others. He tutors us about the idolatry of passing judgment as if we were God rather than a child of God. He teaches us how to respond and then empowers us to that end as this chapter shows.

2. For full treatment of Dr. Fuller's analogy see Daniel P. Fuller, *Gospel and Law* (Grand Rapids, MI: 1980) p. 117-120.
3. This quote has sometimes been attributed to Thomas Adams.

4. The condition is really one of faith. Forgiving others is one way saving faith expresses its confidence in God. For example, if I say, "I have talent!" your immediate question will be, "How does this talent reveal itself? What do you do that shows you have talent?" If I say, "I just have it inside me," you will consider it a very strange claim. In the same way, James argues, "Show me your faith without deeds, and I will show you my faith by what I do" (James 2:18). Forgiving others is one of the talents of saving faith. It shows we are trusting in God's promise of Romans 12:19: "It is mine to avenge; I will repay."

5. Gary Thomas, "A Proper Double Standard," *World*, February 3, 1996, p. 26.

6. Irina Ratushinskaya, *Grey Is the Color of My Hope* (New York: Alfred A. Knopf, 1988).

7. Corrie ten Boom and Jamie Buckingham, *Tramp for the Lord* (Old Tappan, N.J.: Revell, 1974), pp. 56-57.

8. Quoted from *National and International Religion Report* 9, no. 6 (March 6, 1995).

Chapter Ten

1. See Nathan Cobb, "Ray Hammond's Sacrifice," *Boston Globe*, June 6, 1996, p. 33.

2. Charles Swindoll, *Improving Your Serve: The Art of Unselfish Living* (Waco, Tex.: Word, 1981).

3. Dietrich Bonhoeffer, *Letters and Papers from Prison* (New York: Macmillan, 1953), p. 136.

4. God told Abraham that His Great Work consisted of all the *peoples* of the earth being blessed. Jesus commissioned us to take the blessing to *all nations* in fulfillment of the Abrahamic promise. There is broad agreement that this does not mean the sovereign countries. The growing consensus is that God has in mind the distinct cultural groups within each country. For example, Nigeria is one sovereign nation, but the different tribes number 426. There are at least 408 distinct languages spoken among them, maybe more. In 1982, a meeting in Lausanne, Switzerland, was held by mission experts to clarify what a people group was and whether the blessing of the gospel had reached people groups to the degree that fulfilled the promise of God. While humbly acknowledging that we don't know for sure, they agreed on some working definitions. A people group "is a significantly large grouping of individuals who perceive themselves to have a common affinity for one another because of their shared language, religion, ethnicity, residence, occupation, class or caste, situation, etc. Or a combination of these." For evangelistic purposes it is "the largest group within which the Gospel can spread as a church planting movement without encountering barriers of understanding or acceptance." They also agreed upon a working definition of an unreached people group: "A group within which there is no indigenous community of believing Christians able to evangelize this people group." See Ralph Winter, "Unreached Peoples: Recent Developments in the Concept," *Frontier Missions* 11, no. 8-9 (1989): 12.

5. These numbers come from a *Missions Frontiers Bulletin* chart developed

from the research data of the Lausanne Statistics Task Force and their chairman, David Barrett, the author of the *World Christian Encyclopedia.* See *Missions Frontiers Bulletin* 18, no. 1-2 (January-February 1996): 5.

6. Ralph Winter, "The Diminishing Task," *Missions Frontiers Bulletin,* June-August, 1991. p. 53.

7. This number comes from David Barrett, the author of the *World Christian Encyclopedia,* and the Lausanne Statistics Task Force. The estimates reflect the number of "serious Christian believers" only, not nominal or cultural identifications of Christianity. Quoted from *Missions Frontiers Bulletin* 15, no. 5-6 (May-June 1993): 6.

8. Herbert Schlossberg, *Called to Suffer, Called to Triumph* (Portland, Oreg.: Multnomah, 1990), pp. 43-44.

9. Earle E. Cairns, *An Endless Line of Splendor* (Wheaton, Ill.: Tyndale, 1986).

10. Ralph Waldo Emerson, "Give All to Love," in *The Mentor Book of Major American Poets,* ed. Williams and Honig (New York: New American Library, 1962), p. 61.

11. Ralph Winter, "World Evangelization by 2000 A.D.—Is It Possible?" USCWM Series # 05-296, copyright 1996, William Carey Library.

12. Robertson McQuilkin, "Living by Vows," *Christianity Today,* Vol. 34, no. 14, Oct. 8, 1990. p. 40.

13. The term *future grace* comes from John Piper, *Future Grace* (Sisters, Oreg.: Multnomah, 1995).

Group Study Guide:

Chapter One: The Christian Experience of God's Forgiveness

1. Alice, Antoinette, and Eva each has her own reasons for needing to learn about God's forgiveness. What draws you to want to learn more about the forgiveness of God and the Christian experience of forgiveness? What particular questions do you have about God's forgiveness?

2. Has anyone ever said to you, "God could never forgive me for what I've done"? Why do people feel this way? Have you ever felt this way?

3. The apostle Paul says it's possible to believe the gospel *in vain* (1 Corinthians 15:2). According to this text, what constitutes a vain or worthless kind of faith? Describe a situation or pattern of behavior where someone's claims are dubious at best.

4. What is the alternative to both hopelessness and false hope? What is the starting point for building a credible and sure hope for the forgiveness of God? Isaiah 1:18 and Jeremiah 31:33-34 are two promises of God. What would faith in these promises cause us to do?

5. What do you think Uriah said to David when they first met in the kingdom of heaven? What might David have said to Uriah? If God can graciously and justly bring these two together, what does that say about our hope to be reconciled to God and to those we've wounded by our selfish behavior?

6. Psalm 51 is David's prayer expressing his heartfelt desire for God's forgiveness and reconciliation. In reading it over, what seems to echo your own heart's desire?

Chapter Two: Forgiveness Desired: Owning Up to Our Guilt

1. According to Colossians 1:21, why do people feel guilty? How does our guilt affect our relationship to God? How can we tell that things between us are not naturally good and friendly—what are some of the signs of our alienation?

2. Why is it so hard for us to admit our own guilt? What are some of the common ways we deny personal responsibility? How honest are you with yourself and others about owning up to your own guilt?

3. C. S. Lewis once said that all men are ruined castles— ruined, but still castles. What do you think he meant? Do you accept the biblical axiom that you are by nature a "sinner"? Why or why not?

4. Which is worse, your woundedness or your waywardness? Which do we spend more time focused on? What does Isaiah's experience (Isaiah 6:1-7) teach us about what our priorities in life ought to be? How would you react if God were to call you before Him as He did Isaiah? What would you say?

5. What in Daniel's prayer (Daniel 9:3-10,19) seems appropriate in your own case?

Chapter Three: Forgiveness Needed: Acknowledging the Justice of God's Judgment

1. According to Romans 1:18-23, what is the central purpose of our life? What is the source of our true and lasting happiness in life? Why is God right to be angry at all mankind? What evil do we commit against God whenever we sin, however we sin?

2. Do all people have an infinite obligation to live for the glory of God? Why or why not? If this is God's starting point to measure our goodness or evil, what is our usual starting point? Why is Romans 14:23 such a shock to our own sense of goodness?

3. Before reading this chapter, what were your impressions of God's wrath, Final Judgment, and hell? How has your understanding changed in light of the biblical testimony?

4. Is God's judgment too severe or are we worse sinners than we thought?

5. David acknowledged the justice of God's judgment in Psalm 51:4 and "repented." How did he do that? According to Romans 2:8, what is it that we are truly repenting *from* when we repent? What are we repenting *to* in repentance? How would the day *after* we repented be different from the day *before* we repented?

Chapter Four: Forgiveness Promised:
Putting Our Hope in God

1. Why is despair so dangerous, even deadly? What does despair make us do? What is the difference between godly sorrow and worldly sorrow? Which experience are you more familiar with? What is the alternative to denial of sin or despair over sin?

2. Many people believe God's love requires Him to forgive everybody, including those who do not believe in, or even acknowledge, Him. How do we know this isn't true? Why can we be certain that God has a heart to forgive? Whom does God forgive?

3. What does it mean to "put your hope in God"? What is God's response to us when we make Him "our hope"?

4. Reading Genesis 22, how can you tell that Abraham put his hope in God? What did he learn by taking his only son up Mount Moriah?

5. What central promise of God are we depending on when we put our hope in God? What else do we rely on God to provide, in addition to forgiveness, when we put our hope in this promise?

6. In what ways has God tested the substance of your faith? In what ways are you trusting, like Abraham, that "the Lord will provide"?

Chapter Five: Forgiveness Revealed: Discovering Christ as Rescuer

1. How does Magalie's experience before the judge mirror our standing before God? How do we know that the incarnation of Jesus Christ was primarily a rescue mission?
2. Why did Jesus come into the world according to Mark 2:15-17? Who, then, are the only people Jesus cannot forgive? Where does this put you? According to Ephesians 2:1-3, what three things does Jesus save us from? How does this expand your understanding of what it means to be "saved"?
3. How familiar are you with the life and teaching of Jesus as recorded in the Gospels? If you've read one of the Gospels recently, what false perceptions did you have about Jesus, prior to reading, that changed as a result of reading His actual words and accounts?
4. Jesus boldly claimed to be a "sinner's" *only* hope in John 14:6. Christian faith makes an exclusive claim to be the only way to experience God's forgiveness and reconciliation (Acts 4:12). Why is this so offensive to people in general? Why is the idea that all roads lead to heaven and that all religions are equally true and good, offensive to the God of the Bible?
5. What does Jesus mean when He says, "He who has been forgiven little loves little"? How does this reverse the effects of shame and guilt?
6. At this point in your life, are you willing to express your hope in God as "faith in Jesus Christ"? Why or why not?

Chapter Six: Forgiveness Justified: Grasping the Truth of the Cross

1. Elie Wiesel's prayer points to the fundamental problem of how a just and holy God can forgive sinners and still be

just and holy. How does the cross of Jesus Christ answer
this problem? What is being reconciled on the cross?
2. How does the Cross fulfill the promise made to Abraham
on Mount Moriah? According to Isaiah 53, why did Christ
have to suffer and die to fulfill God's promise?
3. What connects us personally to the benefits of the Cross?
Regarding our sin, what two things does our faith believe
were accomplished on the cross on our behalf?
4. What does it mean to be "justified by faith"? Why is God
just to be merciful to repentant sinners? How does this turn
our hope in God into a strong assurance of God's loving-
kindness?
5. What does the resurrection of Jesus affirm according to the
Bible? How did the realization that Christ is alive and reigning define for the apostle Paul what it meant to trust in
Christ? What does he mean when he says, "I have been
crucified with Christ" (Galatians 2:20)? According to
Romans 6, how do we experience our own death and resurrection?
6. Why is God's forgiveness and reconciliation called the gift
of God in Ephesians 2:8-9? What are the attributes of genuine saving faith according to Colossians 1:21-23?

Chapter Seven: Forgiveness Experienced: Cleansing a Stained Conscience

1. Many Christians continue to struggle with persistent shame
and guilt over past behavior. How do we know that God
wants to set us free from this burden? In what ways does the
Bible teach us that Christ died to cleanse our consciences?
2. In Romans 8 the apostle Paul shows us how to fight for a
clean conscience and defend against feelings of condemnation and shame. What truths do we need to stand on in
wrestling with guilt and shame?
3. Why is persistent shame a true threat to Christian faith? How
does persistent shame negatively affect us and those we love?
4. What might you say to someone who says, "I know God
forgives me, but I can't forgive myself"?

5. What is the true and only unforgivable sin? How do we turn from it?

6. When is shame medicinal and proper rather than destructive and belittling to the sufficiency of Christ's death for sin?

7. A clean conscience expresses itself in at least six ways. Discuss these six from your own experience. Which of them is the next step in your obtaining a clean conscience?

Chapter Eight: Forgiveness Enjoyed: Living Under the Influence of Grace

1. According to Ezekiel 36:25-26 and Jeremiah 31:31-34, what does God's true grace accomplish over time in those God forgives? How does this differ from what some people are seeking when they ask for God's grace? In what ways has the powerful influence of God's grace begun to work these promised changes in your own life?

2. How do you take time to "enjoy God and praise His name"? What common difficulties do we face in experiencing joyful and God-glorifying worship? How has God helped you overcome them? What Scriptures have most assisted you in the glad worship of God?

3. The Bible also includes the book of Lamentations and psalms of brokenness, tears, and grief. How do these fit into our worship of God? According to James 4:1-10, when is it more appropriate to weep than rejoice?

4. How is obedience a sign of true faith in God? What are we to make of professing Christians who are persistently disobedient? Would you assure them or warn them?

5. First John was written to give true Christians assurance and false Christians doubt. Do you have a strong sense of assurance that you are under God's grace? Accordingly, how may you know that you are truly a child of God? What assurances has God given to the children of God?

Chapter Nine: Forgiveness Shared: Pushing Past Grudges

1. Why do people nurse their grudges for so long? What benefits do we gain by doing so? Why does God warn us away

from bitterness in Hebrews 12:14-15?

2. In Matthew 18:21-35 Jesus teaches us why forgiving others is one of the conditions for receiving God's free grace. Why is this just and fair? How is this condition in keeping with the rule of salvation by faith alone? What is our faith trusting and depending on God for when we forgive those who've wounded us? How did Jesus demonstrate this faith?

3. The people we live and work with are often like sand in the eye. How can we live graciously with irritating people?

4. In learning to forgive those who've hurt us, God reminds us of His sovereignty. What are we believing when we ascribe sovereignty to God? What "good" do you think God might be working in and through the trouble and sufferings that you have endured?

5. Whom do you need to forgive? What is your plan of action to get past this pain that has been caused you, and the anger and resentment that has resulted? What would it mean to "bless" those who have sinned against you and do "good" for them?

Chapter Ten: Forgiveness Unsheathed: Serving in the Great Work

1. According to Titus 2:14, what is the gospel and what transforming experience results? Where are you on the continuum at present? According to Ephesians 2:10, what are we "saved" in order to do with our new lives?

2. In what way can serving God be demeaning to God, according to Paul in Acts 17:24-25? How does Peter tell us (1 Peter 4:11) we can serve God in a way that honors and glorifies His power and purposes in the world?

3. What are some of the various ways we can serve the living God? Survey Psalm 82, Isaiah 58, Matthew 25:31-46, 1 Corinthians 12, James 1:27.

4. What gifts of service and doors of opportunities do you have for serving in the Great Work? Faith, hope, and love are mentioned in 1 Thessalonians 1:3. How do these things characterize our service in the Great Work of God?

Author

John Ensor is the President and Executive Director of *A Woman's Concern*, Pregnancy Resource Centers. With offices in Boston, Needham and Revere, MA, he connects the Christian community, with their biblical wisdom, practical resources and love, to young women in pregnancy distress. Prior to that he was the pastor of two churches in Boston and continues to preach in many guest pulpits. He is an ordained Baptist minister, with degrees from Gordon-Conwell Theological Seminary and Bethel College (St. Paul). He and his wife, Kristen, and their three children, Nathanael, Megan and Elliot, live in Boston.